LORD,
HEAL MY
HURTS

— B O O K S   B Y   K A Y   A R T H U R —

Lord, I'm Torn Between Two Masters
Lord, I Want to Know You
Lord, Is It Warfare? Teach Me to Stand
Lord, Where Are You When Bad Things Happen?
Lord, Only You Can Change Me
Lord, I Need Grace to Make It Today
Lord, Teach Me to Pray in 28 Days
God, Are You There? Do You Care? Do You Know About Me?
How to Study Your Bible Precept upon Precept
The International Inductive Study Series
Beloved: From God's Heart to Yours
His Imprint, My Expression
To Know Him by Name
As Silver Refined
Our Covenant God
Search My Heart, O God
A Sanctuary for Your Soul
My Savior, My Friend
A Moment with God
With an Everlasting Love
Marriage Without Regrets
Discover 4 Yourself Inductive Bible Studies for Kids

LORD,
HEAL MY
HURTS

A DEVOTIONAL STUDY

on GOD'S CARE *and* DELIVERANCE

KAY
ARTHUR

WATERBROOK
PRESS

LORD, HEAL MY HURTS
PUBLISHED BY WATERBROOK PRESS
2375 Telstar Drive, Suite 160
Colorado Springs, Colorado 80920
A division of Random House, Inc.

ISBN 1-57856-440-9
    (previously 0-88070-879-4)

Printed in the United States of America
2000—First WaterBrook Press Edition

10 9 8 7 6 5 4 3 2 1

CONTENTS

Heal me, O LORD,

and I will be healed;

Save me and I will be saved,

For Thou art my praise.

JEREMIAH 17:14

INTRODUCTION

We are reeling in pain. It's a hurt that runs deep, a hurt that doesn't ever seem to go away. The memory of the things done to us or by us stunts our growth, cripples our walk, infects our relationships. And we think this is the way it will always be. We'll never be whole, never be what we could have been if we hadn't been hurt the way we were.

Possibly you have gone from counselor to counselor, yet deep inside the wounds still fester, seeping their poison into the depths of your being. The venom affects your thinking, your reasoning. You live with "if onlys" and "what ifs," and you covet the lives of others who have not walked the dark corridors that you have walked.

Will relief never come? Will the scars continue to mar the beauty of what might have been? Will relationships with others always be skewed because of where you have been or what has been done to you?

It need not be, Beloved, for God's name is Jehovah-rapha—He is the Lord God who heals. And through this devotional study, He is able to send His Word and heal you from all your distresses. He has done it for thousands upon thousands who have learned these precepts and ordered their lives accordingly, and He will do it for you. That is why this devotional study was written. It has stood the test of time and brought healing in the worst of situations—and all because of what His Word says about our hurts.

I cannot wait to see and to hear what God does again as you cry, "Heal me, O Lord, and I will be healed…save me, O God, and I will be saved." His ear is open to our cry, His mighty arm ready to rescue, His potter's hands ready to reshape us and make our scars part of His exquisite design—one of beauty.

This is a study, Beloved, that you must *do*. This is not a book simply to be read. It won't work without the doing—the participating—the allowing of His healing Word to take hold in your heart and mind. So study well. Study prayerfully. Study expectantly. And watch the healing that will come as you believe your God and do what He says.

It is a study you can do alone—in fact, *Lord, Heal My Hurts* is often assigned to individuals by Christian counselors as part of their counseling. But it is also a study that can be done in groups and even become a ministry for you, Beloved of God, as you desire to reach the hurting of this world and see them healed. If there is that possibility of your using this as a group study in which you would be a facilitator, then read "Guidelines for Group Use" in the "Study Resources" section at the back of this book, where you'll find other valuable tools to enhance this study.

For many, the blessing of this study has been enhanced by the companion video and audio teaching tapes. For more information on these, simply call Precept Ministries International at our toll-free number (1-800-763-8280) and let one of our staff members help you. It would be their pleasure. We also provide training if you would like to develop your skills in handling the Word of God more accurately or in leading others in group studies designed to minister to people of all ages at any level of commitment while respecting the restraints on their time. We're known as "The Inductive Study People: everybody, everywhere, any time, any place, any language, any age. One message: the Bible. One method: inductive." Please don't hesitate to call us.

Finally, let me share my vision—it's the possibility of a new avenue of ministry for you, Beloved of God...

A new beginning—
An avenue of ministry—
A sense of doing something that has eternal value

These are three things I think are so important for you and for me. There's so much to learn, to know, to experience, to do—and we never want to lose sight of that. To do so would be to miss what God has for us. To fall short of the tremendous potential of our lives—a potential that is ours because we are His, because we are children of the Creator of the

Universe, indwelt by His divine Spirit and given the mind of Christ. You and I, Beloved, are God's workmanship gifted by the Spirit of God and created in Christ Jesus unto good works that would absolutely stagger our minds if we were to see them before they ever happened.

And what has God put into your hands? What are you holding and reading right now? Is it an accident? A coincidence? No! You are holding a devotional study that first and foremost will be the beginning of a new depth of understanding about God's deep healing that is available for every hurt we have ever known.

God is going to speak to you because through this book you are going to come face to face with the living Word of God—the Word that not only discerns the thoughts and intentions of your heart, but becomes the means of throwing His light on the direction your life is taking so you can know with absolute confidence where you are headed. If you listen to what He says—and by that I mean ordering your life accordingly—then there is, in a sense, a new beginning...of understanding, of purpose. A new level of Christlikeness is attained. You will be, as Paul would say, pressing on and attaining that for which Jesus Christ laid hold of you.

Which brings me to my next point—an avenue of ministry. What you have learned, God intends for you to share. I have a vision, and you, Beloved, are part of that vision. Our Lord's commission in Matthew 28 was that we make disciples of all men—that we teach them to observe all that He has commanded us. Acts 1 tells us that when we are saved and receive the Holy Spirit we become His witnesses—yet the question is often, "How?"

Here is the how. This "Lord" book contains truths every human being needs to know and to apply to his or her life. These are precepts for life; through them we will gain understanding and, as the psalmist says, "hate every false way" (Psalm 119:104). We hate it because it is false rather than true, and it is truth that sets us apart, sets us free.

So what is my vision for you, my friend? It is that you go to the Lord in prayer and ask Him to direct you to at least one other person—but preferably at least ten—and that you, along with them, study this book together. You may not be a teacher, but you can be the group's facilitator. You can take the questions you'll find at the end of each chapter and use them to stimulate a discussion among those whom the Lord has brought together in answer to your prayer. These are those who will be part of your crown of rejoicing in the presence of our Lord Jesus Christ. As you watch them learn and grow in the knowledge of God and of His Word, you will experience the humbling joy of knowing that you have been used of God. That what you have done has eternal value. That your life and God-given gifts have not been wasted. That your work will live on—that the grace of God poured out on you was not poured out in vain, for you have labored in the strength of His grace.

So as you facilitate a group using this book, you need to watch for and encourage others in your group to do as you have done—to take what they have learned and impart it to another as you did with them. Think of the multiplication that will happen! Do you realize, Beloved, that this is the way we can reach our neighborhoods, our communities, our nation, and beyond? Think of the transformation that will take place among all those people today who are so interested in "the spiritual" but won't step inside a church. Think—just think!—what is going to happen!

The time is now. The hour is short. Stop and pray right now and ask God what He would have you to do. He will show you, because He is God and because such prayers are in accordance with His will. As you step out and begin, just know that if you will step out in faith, God will give you an avenue of ministry, person by person or group by group, that will not only stagger your mind but absolutely delight your soul.

I cannot wait to hear what God does in and through you, my friend.

Kay

WHY AM I HURTING?

My platinum wedding band rolled round and round on the rec room floor, making a mockery of what was taking place. Tom was on the floor, groping, looking for my diamond engagement ring in the shadows of the table lamps. As I stood in the corner of the room, looking on the scene like a detached spectator, my lips were taut. No crying. No more hysterical sobbing. I was beyond that. As far as I was concerned, it was over.

The wedding band had finally stopped spinning in circles. It lay dormant—just like our marriage. Tom was still looking for the engagement ring. I had thrown it at him along with my wedding band. He was murmuring something about how expensive the ring was. That made me sick!

I thought, *You care more about that stupid, expensive diamond ring than you do about me! Don't you know what has happened? I have taken off my wedding band! The one you had engraved with the words 'Our Love Is Eternal.' Don't you realize—hasn't it occurred to you, Tom Goetz—that it has never been off my hand since the day of our wedding?*

The quarrel had begun in our bedroom. I didn't want to go back, so I stayed downstairs. For the first time in our six years of marriage, Tom had slapped me. I'd cut him down with my tongue. It was too much for him. He just couldn't handle it. He lost control. As the warm, salty blood from my nose touched my lips, I told Tom it was over—finished. He had followed me downstairs, pleading. Now he went to bed, alone.

Whether Tom slept or not, I don't know. I only know that the next day we called our priest. It was cut and dried. He thought we ought to separate. I would take our young sons, Tom and Mark, and move back to Arlington, Virginia, where I had friends. It was that simple—on the outside. Inside an unseen but very real wound began to fester. Its poison slowly began seeping into my soul. If the wound had been mine alone, it wouldn't have been nearly as bad. I didn't know how badly the boys were hurting...they never cried in front of me.

My friend, have you ever contemplated divorce?

Have you ever wanted to walk away from a relationship? To say, "Forget it; it's not worth it"?

Have you ever hurt so badly that you thought the pain would never go away? That it would be easier to die?

Or have you ever been so horribly hurt that you wished, or even prayed, that the person who had hurt you would just die?

Are you hurting...emotionally, spiritually, psychologically? Or do you have a mate, a child, a relative, or a friend who hurts?

What's the answer, the solution? Is there one? Are some condemned to hurt forever? Are there some who have wounds so great that they can never be healed? Or *is* there healing for what hurts...no matter how bad the hurt?

There is. Whether you believe it or not, you are beloved of God. He desires your wholeness, your healing. About twenty-five hundred years ago, God had the prophet Jeremiah record His burden for His people who were hurting.

Listen to the anguish of Jeremiah's heart: "For the brokenness of the daughter of my people I am broken; I mourn, dismay has taken hold of me" (Jeremiah 8:21).

Why the anguish? Was it because of the greatness of their wound? No, Beloved, it was because there was a cure for their hurts, and they were unaware of it. Or perhaps it was because they knew where to turn but refused for some reason or the other.

Listen to Jeremiah's cry of dismay: "Is there no balm in Gilead? Is there no physician there? Why then has not the health of the daughter of my people been restored?" (Jeremiah 8:22).

A balm in Gilead…a physician there…and healing for every wound of your soul! This, my friend, is what this devotional study is all about.

I cannot wait to see, and hopefully to hear, what God does through this study in relation to healing what hurts you. Study diligently. You will be awed by what God will do as you believe His Word and live accordingly. I know. I have been healed, and so have many, many others.

May I make a suggestion? Find the book of Jeremiah in your Bible. If you don't know where it is, there is a table of contents in the front of the Bible. Look under the Old Testament books until you see Jeremiah and the page number on which it begins. Now, why don't you read a chapter or two? As you do, ask God to give you understanding regarding His people whom He refers to as Judah and what they were experiencing and why. If you are new to the Bible, don't let reading it overwhelm you. You will find yourself learning more and more about the Bible as we progress through our quest for healing.

— D A Y   T W O —

I never thought I would go through a divorce. There had always been only one thing I ever wanted in life, and that was to be happily married for ever and ever…just like my mom and dad.

I wanted to be wildly in love…just like in the movies. I wanted an all-American husband who loved his wife and children. I wanted us all to live happily ever after. I would have been content to stay at home, to be the wife of a successful businessman. To raise my all-American boys, to dance away the weekends in the arms of my husband, laughing and enjoying the company of our friends.

Now after six years of marriage, the dream was over. My dream had become a nightmare. And it hurt. I had failed. The one and only thing I had ever wanted—to be happily married to one man until death parted us at an old age—was over. It had come and gone. I was only twenty-six years old.

Oh it hurt! But not as badly as it was going to! I was so self-centered, so bent on my own happiness that I never really comprehended how badly it had hurt Tom. He didn't want a divorce. We just followed bad advice given by someone in a clerical collar. Once we were separated, the divorce seemed to follow naturally.

Tom hated living alone. He would call me and tell me that he was going to a psychiatrist. When I asked why, he said that he couldn't forget the awful things I had said to him.

From time to time when we talked, he would tell me that he was going to commit suicide. Thinking I would bluff him out of it, I would say, "Go ahead. But do a good job so I get your money!" His hurt became a wound—a wound that would go deeper with every phone call, every letter. Deeper until he put a rope around his neck. He died, his hurt never healed. Never able to hear my cry of "I'm sorry! If only I had known…"

For me, it would be different. One day I would cry out, "Heal me, O Lord, and I will be healed! Save me, O Lord, and I will be saved!" I would discover that there was a balm in Gilead that could heal the sin-sick soul. How I wish I could have shared what I learned with Tom!

All of my hurt—living with Tom's suicide, coping with the memories of failing my two sons by divorcing their father and exposing them to my ensuing immorality—would be healed by this same balm and by my Great Physician whom I would come to know as Abba, Father.

I have a message for you, beloved reader. One of hope, of life, of peace. Not my message, not psychology's, but God's! Whatever your wound, your hurt—whether it is mostly a self-inflicted wound like mine or whether it is a wound inflicted by others—God's Word says that there is a balm in Gilead, that there is a Great Physician there. And because that is true, you can cry out, "Heal me, O LORD, and I will be healed; save me and I will be saved, for Thou art my praise" (Jeremiah 17:14).

I believe any child of God can be healed of the deepest, most horrendous wounds if he will learn three things: how to apply the balm of Gilead, how to follow the Great Physician's instructions, and how to give His medicine time to work. And that is what our study will be all about. In the days to come, the term the *balm of Gilead* will take on meaning and deep significance as you learn how this phrase was used in Old Testament days.

May I suggest, my friend, that today you shut yourself up with the Lord for a little while and ask Him to show you if there are any hurts in your life, past or present, for which you need healing. As God shows them to you, write them down.

If you feel fine—no hurts, past or present—then write out your mate's hurts or your friends' hurts.

As you write, please don't worry about what anyone would think. This is your workbook. Seeing your thoughts in black and white will help you define them. When you are instructed to write something out, you will find it very helpful to do exactly that. There will always be a reason for what I will ask you to do, and I believe it will all be helpful.

When you finish writing out your thoughts, look up Jeremiah 17:14, and write it out below. Then memorize it. I have found that the easiest way to memorize something is to read it aloud three times in succession morning, afternoon, and evening. Try it!

Heal me, O Lord, and I will be aled, save me and I will be saved you are the one I praise

— D A Y   T H R E E —

"My sorrow is beyond healing, my heart is faint within me!" (Jeremiah 8:18). Did Jeremiah pen these words to describe only his anguish as he mourned over the awful ravages of sin in the lives of his people? No, as it says in Roman 15:4, "For whatever was written in earlier times was written for our instruction, that through perseverance and the encouragement of the Scriptures we might have hope."

My friend, after having taken a look at the hurts in your life or in the life of your mate or a friend, do you feel a sorrow that you believe may be beyond healing? Do you feel that wholeness is an impossibility? That healing is a miracle that could never happen?

Are the words from Jeremiah 8:18 your words? Could you have written them yourself? Do you sometimes wonder how you can go on? If life will ever be more than mere existence and day-by-day survival? Or are there times when you wish you wouldn't survive? When death would be welcome if you didn't have to do it yourself or if you could be sure that death would really be sweeter, more bearable than life?

I understand. For the most part, I caused my wounds. And yet whether I inflicted them on myself through my selfish and willful disobedience to the precepts of God or whether another inflicted them upon me, my wounds hurt.

Although the cause of our pain may not be the same, I have held countless numbers of hurting, bruised, wounded people in my arms. I have wept with and prayed with people who were so emotionally and physically abused that, if I had not known the healing power of the Word of God, I would have said, "There is no hope!" I have read their letters, and their pain was so great that at times I thought my heart would break.

There is nothing new under the sun. Some wounds may be deeper, more extensive, but pain is pain, hurt is hurt—it all throbs.

The wounds others have shared with me have run the gamut of hurt—from thoughts of worthlessness and hopelessness to feeling dirty, used, and cast off. Some have been so abused sexually, physically, and emotionally that they are tormented by the memories—plagued by anything that recalls the incidents to the screens of their thoughts. The horrors of the incidents of the past, the inability to cope, the feelings of never being good enough overwhelm and incapacitate them. They live with "if onlys"—"if only I had never married him or her...if only I hadn't allowed myself...if only I had responded differently...if only..."

And I understand. Don't you? Haven't you, too, allowed your mind to rehash the past, wondering what could have been "if only"? It's hell, isn't it? There is constant torment as you go over and over it all in your mind. I know. I have been there, but I have also found God's healing.

Although sharing what happened with Tom reawakens pain and brings tears to my eyes, I can go on. I can live as more than a conqueror. And so can you, my friend. God has a way of escape, and we are going to find it.

Today, go to the Lord in prayer and let Him know exactly how you feel at this point about His ability to heal you. Again, I believe writing out your thoughts will help. Don't be embarrassed. God already knows your thoughts. However, as you address God directly with your thoughts and feelings, it becomes open communication which then can be dealt with in a way God designed. That way is prayer.

— D A Y   F O U R —

In the days of Jeremiah, the people of the southern kingdom of Judah found themselves in a distressing state. They were broken by the ravages of sin. Much like our day, sin had taken its devastating toll, touching every level of society from commoner to priest to prophet to king. Judah was a broken nation of wounded people because of their sin and because of the effects of their sin upon society.

Some went about proclaiming, "Peace, peace," but there was no peace. They looked for healing, but it eluded them. What was the problem? Let's look at it today because as we do, we will eventually see God's answer. The solution offered in Jeremiah's day is the same solution God offers for every age.

Before you begin reading Jeremiah, let me give you the historical context of the book. Until the death of Solomon, David's son, the nation of Israel had been one kingdom with Jerusalem as its capital. Then when Solomon's son, Rehoboam, came to power, the kingdom divided into the northern and southern kingdoms. Under Jeroboam, ten tribes formed the northern kingdom, eventually making Samaria their capital. This northern kingdom, which went under the name Israel, no longer had access to the temple at Jerusalem. Thus they made themselves two golden calves, built an altar, and set up their own system of worship. Their idolatry continued until about 722 B.C. when God sent the Assyrians down to take them captive.

The southern kingdom of Judah was comprised of the two tribes of Judah and Benjamin. Although Judah saw God's judgment upon her sister, Israel, she didn't learn from Israel's mistakes. In the final days of Jeremiah, God allowed the Babylonians (Chaldeans) to take Judah captive in 586 B.C. The book of Jeremiah describes the awful brokenness of this nation, the call of God to repentance through Jeremiah, and the ultimate destruction of Judah because they would not listen and be healed.

In light of that brief history, read the first two chapters of Jeremiah.

Watch how God talks to Judah, reminding her of the days when He became her God (which, of course, was when Israel became a kingdom and before the kingdom split).

After you read these two chapters, look up the following verses from Jeremiah and summarize what you learn about the situation in Judah during Jeremiah's time. As you record your observations, see if there are any parallels to our day. You might want to write the parallel in a second color of ink so that you can easily recognize it.

1. Jeremiah 2:1-8

2. Jeremiah 2:13 (Note the comparisons or contrasts in this verse.)

3. Jeremiah 2:17-19

4. Jeremiah 2:20-25

— D A Y   F I V E —

Before we look at the solution to Judah's hurt, I want you to read more in Jeremiah. If ever there were a book Christians need to study at this time in history, it is Jeremiah. If you will read it from the perspective of how the situation in Judah parallels the state of affairs in your nation today, you will find yourself awed at the similarities. I hope you will also become determined not to respond to the Word of God in the same way.

Read through Jeremiah 3–5, and then we'll walk through it together. Please don't let this overwhelm you. Believe me, I don't want you to

become discouraged in any way. I don't want you to miss the healing that
will be yours if you will only persevere through these thirteen weeks.

Our study will be a process. You will not find instant relief in a "one-
two-three steps and you're healed" type of teaching. I'm convinced there
are some crucial, fundamental truths which must be the basis of your healing, if your healing is going to be more than superficial. So hangeth thou
in there!

Now then, let's walk together through Jeremiah, taking it one point at
a time.

1. In Jeremiah 3 God shows how His wife, "faithless Israel," has played
   the harlot.
   a. Read Jeremiah 3:1-13.
   b. List what you learned about Israel's behavior in the following
      verses:
      (1) 3:1

      (2) 3:6,13 (The heathen practices of worship in those days often
      involved giving homage to trees which were cut in phallic [sexual]
      symbols.)

2. In Jeremiah 4:19-22 you can almost hear Jeremiah wail in anguish as he sees God's judgment approaching through war and captivity. Read these verses and note what you observe about the people.

3. In Jeremiah 5:7 God asks a very valid question: "Why should I pardon you?" There are many reasons why He shouldn't. These are given in chapter 5. Read the chapter and list those reasons and the verses in which you found them. Then in the second column, list the parallels to today.

REASONS FOR GOD'S JUDGMENT   PARALLELS TO TODAY

God didn't want to judge Israel, even though He had just reasons for doing so. Throughout the book of Jeremiah, God calls the people to listen and to return to Him: "'Return, faithless Israel,' declares the LORD; 'I will not look upon you in anger. For I am gracious,' declares the LORD; 'I will not be angry forever. Only acknowledge your iniquity, that you have transgressed against the LORD your God and have scattered your favors to the strangers under every green tree, and you have not obeyed My voice,' declares the LORD" (Jeremiah 3:12-13).

As you study Jeremiah, you may relate to faithless Israel because you have not loved God as you should or because you have not lived for Him as you should have lived. If you haven't already, acknowledge your sin. My friend, know that God is still standing there in mercy, waiting for you to cry in faith, "Heal me, O LORD, and I will be healed; save me and I will be saved" (Jeremiah 17:14).

Turn and run into those outstretched arms of Calvary's love. He will heal you.

– D A Y   S I X –

Have you ever wondered how some individuals can get so messed up? How can fathers and mothers give birth to children and then misuse or abuse them? How can they abuse them verbally? How can a parent reject a child? Be mean to him? Abandon him?

How can fathers sexually assault their infant daughters? It is hard to comprehend. We don't even want to think about it because it is so abhorrent. Yet, it goes on far more often than most people realize.

Why do parents lash out at their children and abuse them emotionally? Why do they knock them around, taking out their anger and frustration on someone who is weaker, smaller than they are? What causes a father to become so emotionally sick that he would do something like this to any child, let alone his own? Have you ever wondered, ever thought about it?

Why do people become dropouts on life? Why do they walk out on relationships? Why do they become drug addicts, alcoholics, prostitutes, homosexuals, lesbians? Why do people get lured into occult practices?

Why do people ruin their lives and the lives of others? Is that what they wanted to do with their lives when they grew up?

I realize that the answer goes back to the problem of inherent sin. And I know that Jesus is the only person ever born who wasn't born in sin (Romans 5:12). However, people long for some semblance of heaven, not hell, in their lives.

When people do not listen to the Word of the Lord, it affects families, which in turn affect societies, which in turn affect nations, which in turn can affect the world. Throughout Jeremiah you read the phrase "yet they did not listen to Me." The source of our problems can be traced back to someone's failure to listen to God, listening so as to believe and obey Him.

Now that may seem simplistic to you, but if you will carefully read the Word of God, you will see that it is true. Sin originally entered into the world because Adam and Eve did not listen to God. Eve listened, instead, to Satan and believed a lie. And what they did affected all future generations.

When I think of my first marriage, I know I went through our divorce and Tom's suicide because I didn't listen to God. I didn't do what He told me to do as a wife and a mother. I did it my way. But you may say to me, "Well, Tom wasn't perfect either! If he had met your needs, then..."

And I would say, "But Tom had hurts from his family..." Then we would trace it all to the fact that Tom's parents didn't listen to God, and Tom, in his trials, didn't listen to God. None of us did! Yet, we all had the opportunity!

Stop for a few minutes, and think about your own wounds, the hurts which you have suffered. Why did they happen? Think about it and write it out.

As I have been writing *Lord, Heal My Hurts,* I have been thinking about you. It occurs to me that maybe you do not know much about the Word of God. Maybe the Bible has been a closed and boring book to you, like it used to be to me. Or maybe you've never even read it. Maybe you have picked up this book because you are hurting and are desperate for relief, I am so glad the Lord has brought us together! If you are genuinely seeking God, you won't be disappointed.

In case you are new to the Bible, I want to define sin for you. Sin began in the Garden of Eden when the first man and woman disobeyed God. God told them not to eat of the fruit of the tree of the knowledge of good and evil. He also told them the consequences if they disobeyed. However, instead of believing and obeying God, they listened to the serpent of old, the devil.

Sin is disobedience. To know the right thing to do and not do it is sin (James 4:17). Whatever is not of faith is sin (Romans 14:23). Therefore, sin is unbelief. Sin is lawlessness (1 John 3:4). Sin is man's turning to his own way. Isaiah 53:6 says, "All of us like sheep have gone astray, each of us has turned to his own way; but the LORD has caused the iniquity of us all to fall on Him."

Now then, let's continue walking through Jeremiah. We will look at chapters 6, 7, and 8. We are on the brink of finding Jeremiah's solution to the hurts of his people!

The solution will be mentioned at the end of our Scripture reading today, but it will not yet be explained. As we go through Jeremiah 6, 7, and 8, take the information you glean and put it on the chart which follows. It will help you if you are doing this study with a discussion group.

1. If you have time, read all of Jeremiah 6. If you don't have time, read at least verses 6-19. Then note what you learn about God's people in verses 7,10,13,14, and 19. Record your insights on the chart.

2. Read Jeremiah 7. When you finish, look up verses 8-10,13,18, 23-28,30,31 and record your observations on the chart.

3. Did you notice in Jeremiah 7:1-7 that God gave them the opportunity to repent? Repent means to have a change of mind. A change of mind regarding the way they were living would result in a change of their lives, wouldn't it?

4. Finally, we come to Jeremiah 8. Once again, it would be to your advantage to read the entire chapter. When you finish, look up Jeremiah 8:5-7,9-12 and record your insights on your chart.

5. Now then, what is the solution to their problems? Or to put it another way, why is Jeremiah dismayed? Read Jeremiah 8:21-22, and record your insights. As I said earlier, you may not understand the significance of Jeremiah's terminology in these verses, but you will later.

IN JEREMIAH'S DAY

THE PROBLEMS   THE PEOPLE'S ATTITUDE

WHAT THEY NEED FOR HEALING

− D A Y   S E V E N −

As many have shared their hurts with me, I have understood how Jeremiah felt when he cried, "For the brokenness of the daughter of my people I am broken; I mourn, dismay has taken hold of me. Is there no balm in Gilead: Is there no physician there? Why then has not the health of the daughter of my people been restored?" (Jeremiah 8:21-22).

Can you sense Jeremiah's anguish? Don't you sense that some of his despair related to the fact that he knew there was a cure, yet he saw the people were not listening?

There is a sure cure. There is a way to be healed, to be whole. I want you to know that. The people of Jeremiah's day didn't have to live in despair and defeat, nor do you. You do not have to be crippled by the trauma of your past any more than the children of Judah did.

I honestly believe, Beloved, that there is no trauma of your past, no wound of your mind, emotions, heart, or soul beyond the healing power of God. Why? There is a balm in Gilead. There is a Great Physician there.

Our study next week will help you see for yourself exactly who the physician is. Then we will take a thorough look at the balm of Gilead. After that we will move on to specific hurts and see how these are to be handled so that there can be a genuine healing.

As Jeremiah looked at the brokenness of the people, dismay overwhelmed him because the people thought they were doomed to a life of total despair. (Maybe you can relate!) The people had forgotten they had a God whose name was Jehovah-rapha, the God who heals. Thus, Jeremiah looked at their awful state and cried, "Is there no balm in Gilead? Is there no physician there?" The assumed, obvious answer was a resounding "YES!" You can tell from the way that Jeremiah asked his next question: "Why then has not the health of the daughter of my people been restored?" (Jeremiah 8:22).

The ultimate source of your total healing—or anyone's—will be the Great Physician and the balm He has ordained. Therefore, won't you close this week by writing out a prayer to God regarding your healing, your mate's healing, or the healing of a friend. Come to God in faith. If your faith is weak, tell God. If you think your healing is beyond His love, care, ability, or power, tell Him. Just communicate. You might want to incorporate Jeremiah 17:14 in your prayer.

Memory Verse

Heal me, O LORD, and I will be healed; save me and I will be saved, for Thou art my praise.

JEREMIAH 17:14

Small-Group Discussion Questions

1. As you read the passages in Jeremiah this week, you saw the broken, wounded state of the people. Why were Jeremiah's people in this state?
2. What are some of the hurts in your life, in the lives of your family, in the lives of your friends?
3. What parallels are there between the time in which Jeremiah lived and the time in which we live?

4. What do you think is the reason for these hurts, for the horrors that we see in our world daily?

5. When we do things our own way and not God's way, what are we doing?

6. In Jeremiah 7:1-7, we see God's heart toward the people as He offers them an opportunity to do what?

7. As you have thought about your hurts, the hurts of others, and the state of our world, do you echo with Jeremiah his cry found in Jeremiah 8:18: "My sorrow is beyond healing, my heart is faint within me"? What is God's answer to this cry, the solution to the problem in Jeremiah's day, in our day?

8. What did you learn from this study that you could apply to your own life?

9. What question did this lesson bring to your thoughts?

RUN TO YOUR
GREAT PHYSICIAN

A re you suffering a bitter situation? Let me tell you of Jehovah-rapha, the Lord who heals by taking the bitter and making it sweet.

Let's study this name for God which shows Him as the one who heals. During Moses' account of the Israelites' exodus from Egypt, *Jehovah-rapha* occurs for the first time in Scripture. The children of Israel had just crossed the Red Sea and Moses had sung his song of victory: "The horse and its rider He has hurled into the sea" (Exodus 15:1). The Israelites had come to Marah where their thirst could not be quenched because the waters of Marah were bitter.

Now that you have the context, we'll look at Exodus 15:22-26 in greater detail.

Then Moses led Israel from the Red Sea, and they went out into the wilderness of Shur; and they went three days in the wilderness and found no water. And when they came to Marah, they could not drink the waters of Marah, for they were bitter; therefore it was named Marah. So the people grumbled at Moses, saying, "What shall we drink?" Then he cried out to the LORD, and the LORD showed him a tree; and he threw it into the waters, and the waters became sweet. There He made for them a statute and regulation, and there He tested them. And He said,

"If you will give earnest heed to the voice of the LORD your God, and do what is right in His sight, and give ear to His commandments, and keep all His statutes, I will put none of the diseases on you which I have put on the Egyptians; for I, the LORD, am your healer."

God was saying, "I am Jehovah-rapha—the one who is your healer." Have you ever seen God in this light?

Like so many today, the children of Israel found themselves drinking bitter water. They didn't know the bitter water was a test. Did you see the word *tested?* Go back and underline it or put a diagram around it.

God wanted the children of Israel to learn an important principle: When things are difficult, you are to run to God. Listening and obeying Him will bring healing. God can take the bitter and make it sweet, because He is our healer.

Compare their situation to yours today. When you have found yourself drinking bitter water, what did you do? To whom did you turn? Take a few minutes and list the various avenues you have taken or followed for healing. State whether or not they worked and why.

— D A Y   T W O —

The physician to whom Jeremiah was referring was God because His name is Jehovah-rapha. Jehovah is the name that reveals God as the self-existent one. This name is significant when it comes to understanding God as the one who can heal you! Since He is the self-existent healer, your healing is not really dependent upon anything other than God.

As you allow yourself to take that truth in, you will breathe a sigh of relief because there are no other factors that have to come together in order for you to be healed! God is the only factor! He is the one who heals (Deuteronomy 32:39).

Just recently I received a letter from a woman who is obviously hurting. She wrote:

Last Friday night you used an illustration in your message about a heavy-set woman who ran down the aisle during one of your messages on forgiveness. She would not forgive her father for the sexual abuse he had put her through. Would you please share with me what you shared with her? I identify with this woman very much. But I never got pregnant. Yet the anger and unforgiveness are still there.

It also extends into my relationship with other males, as I cannot form a friendship relationship with other males. I'm thirty-seven and I can't get past this. But more important it causes serious problems with my relationship with the Lord. The word *father* is not a good word. I hate it. When I try to pray I see myself standing in front of the Lord like I used to stand in front of my father. I realize the problem, but I don't know how to get past it. I love the Lord, but I don't trust Him. How do I get to trust and let those tall, thick walls down?

This letter could have been written by any one of thousands of women. How can they begin to be healed when the damage has been so great? How could they ever trust God when their image of a father has been so perverted and twisted by their own fathers?

Some would tell you that these women could never be completely whole. Others would say healing wouldn't come without years of professional counseling. But is this true?

No, it's not. God's name is Jehovah-rapha—the God who heals. The God who is in the process of healing the woman abused by her father is the same God who can heal you.

Think about it.

— D A Y   T H R E E —

In the Greek language[1] the word we translate as *rapha* means "to mend, to cure." It is translated "to heal, repair, repair thoroughly, make whole." It is translated *physicians* in Genesis 50:2: "And Joseph commanded his servants the physicians to embalm his father. So the physicians embalmed Israel."

Sometimes we think of healing only in the realm of physical healing, but does God heal only physical diseases? Rather than tell you no and have you take my word for it, I want you to search God's Word for yourself.

The symbol for the ministry I represent, Precept Ministries International, is a plumb line. A plumb line is an instrument by which you discern what is straight. The Word of God is our plumb line. If what we think or believe does not agree with the Word of God, then we know we are off the track of truth. God's Word is truth (John 17:17).

Now look up the following references and note what or whom the Lord heals. In some instances you may need to check the context of the verse. The context is the surrounding verses.

1. Deuteronomy 32:39

2. Isaiah 19:22

3. Isaiah 57:17-18

4. Psalm 147:3

5. Isaiah 30:26

6. Isaiah 53:5 with 1 Peter 2:24-25

7. Genesis 20:17

8. Acts 10:38

In light of what you have observed from the Word of God so far, do you think there's anything out of the realm of God's healing power? If so, be honest and record it. Then in the days to come, we'll see what God has to say.

— D A Y   F O U R —

Let's review what you have learned about the Great Physician. If God's name is Jehovah-rapha, the God who heals, then that is what God does: He heals. And He can heal you. God's name is as good as God's person. His name stands because He never changes. God is the same yesterday, today, and forever (Hebrews 13:8). He has always been, and He always will be, Jehovah-rapha.

Beloved, to whom have you run for healing? Make sure that you get godly counsel—that which has its very foundation in the Word of God, that which points you to God and all that He is—rather than counsel that is apart from Him and His precepts of life. Don't think that the spiritual part of you belongs to God and, thus, can be healed by God, while the psychological part must be healed through man's wisdom. The One who created you, who formed you—body, soul, and spirit—is not only your creator, He is also your sustainer.

1. Write out Jeremiah 17:5-6.

2. Now write out Jeremiah 17:7-8.

3. To solidify this contrast between the cursed and the blessed, either draw a picture showing the differences between them or list the differences between them.

THE CURSED   THE BLESSED

My staff and I have talked with many people who have gone to professional counselors and in the process have spent hours of their time and hundreds or thousands of dollars, yet they are still living like a dried-up bush in the desert. Their counselors never led them to the Word of God to find the solution. They received counsel from man, but it didn't resolve their conflict because man could only deal with the problem from man's perspective.

We have had the opportunity to take them to the Word of God, to teach them about the character and ways of God, to help them see the necessity of total surrender to Jesus Christ as Lord. In the process of bathing them in the truths of God's Word, we have seen them healed. Hallelujah means "praise be to Jehovah or Jah"…and we say, "Hallelujah!"

– D A Y   F I V E –

When you examine Jeremiah 8 carefully, you see that Jeremiah was dismayed over the brokenness of God's people. There was a balm in Gilead. There was a Physician there. But his people had failed to take advantage of either. Their wound was curable, but they were not accepting God's cure. In their trials and testings, they ran to everyone but God. Therefore, their wounds were healed superficially.

They listened to every prophet who came down the road proclaiming his dreams and visions, but they would not pay attention to God's commandments. A repeated phrase in Jeremiah is "But you did not listen." Because they did not listen to God, they missed the balm of Gilead.

In Gilead they produced a salve known for its healing and cosmetic properties. "The balm of Gilead" had become a proverbial phrase synonymous with healing. Thus, the Lord spoke through Jeremiah saying, "Go up to Gilead and obtain balm, O virgin daughter of Egypt! In vain have you multiplied remedies; there is no healing for you" (Jeremiah 46:11). The people of Judah had acted just like the world. They tried to find healing for themselves, but there was no healing apart from God.

What a parallel! So many have run to Egypt—a picture of the world and all that it has to offer. There they try to find healing for their wounded souls when they should have run to God as their Jehovah-rapha. They should have sought out God's counsel and cure for their hurts. But they didn't! It was easier to listen to man, whom they could see, than to listen to God, whom they could not see, who seemed so far removed from man and his needs.

In Jeremiah's day the word of God had become a reproach to His people (Jeremiah 29:19; 42:13; 43:4; 44:16-17). The whole nation, for the most part, was sick from the top of their heads to the tip of their toes. There was no healing for them because "from the prophet even to the priest everyone practices deceit. And they heal the brokenness of the daughter of My people superficially, saying, 'Peace, peace' but there is no peace" (Jeremiah 8:10-11).

The prophets prophesied falsely. The priests ruled on their own authority. And God's people loved it (Jeremiah 5:31). And the end of it all was awful. The people were never healed.

To describe their almost hopeless condition, God metaphorically tells His people that they have forsaken the living water of the Word of God for the filthy waters of the Nile. Instead of going to Gilead where they could find refuge and God's means of healing, they went to Assyria and drank the waters of the Euphrates (Jeremiah 2:14-19).

What they did in Jeremiah's day, we have done in ours. Many have drunk the waters of psychology, philosophy, and psychiatry instead of drinking the Water of Life. We have run to men and women trained in the world's wisdom, but we have not run in prayer to the child that was born, the son that was given, whose name is "Wonderful Counselor, Mighty God, Eternal Father, Prince of Peace" (Isaiah 9:6).

All of this is not to say that we should not go to others for help. Rather we should not fail to go to God. And when we turn to others, what real and lasting help can they give us if their counsel is contrary to God's Word?

Stop and think about it. Where do you turn first in the time of hurt, of need, of doubt? Write it out.

If you wrote "to God," let me ask, What do you do when you turn to Him? Do you wait on Him to see what He will put upon your heart? Do you seek Him through the counsel of His Word?

God ministers through His Word. As you read His Word daily, you will find Him speaking to you in incredible ways, miraculously supplying just what you need for that specific time—or bringing to your remembrance what you have already read.

If, however, you wrote that you turn to alcohol, to pills, to drugs, to promiscuity, let me say that these will not help you. They will simply escort you into oblivion as they lead you into sin's bondage…into slavery and destruction.

Beloved, run to your Jehovah-rapha.

— D A Y   S I X —

As we talk about running to the arm of flesh in our distress, in our times of need, I can't help but think about King Asa of Judah.

Read 2 Chronicles 14. When you finish reading, answer the following questions:

1. What was Asa's relationship with the Lord like?

2. When the Ethiopians came against Asa, what did Asa do?

3. What did God do?

Read 2 Chronicles 15. (I don't want to wear you out, but hangeth thou in there; it will be worth it!)

4. What was God's warning to Asa?

5. How did Asa respond?

Finally, read 2 Chronicles 16.

6. When Asa found himself confronted by the King of Israel, what did he do?

7. How did God feel about this? How do you know?

8. What kind of a man or woman is God searching for? And what will be the benefits of being such a man or woman?

Like King Asa of Judah, many have physicians instead of the Lord (2 Chronicles 16:12). They are not being healed—or they are being treated superficially with Band-Aids.

Who is to blame?

— *D A Y   S E V E N* —

Are you a victim of abuse? Have you been taken advantage of by man so that you are a distortion of what God intended? Was your childhood raped of its innocence?

Do you feel caught in a web of sin woven out of the threads of rejection, anger, fear, and bitterness? Have you been told that you will never be free—that it's impossible to ever be the same?

Have you been told that you will be maimed for life? That you will always be an emotional cripple, never completely well, never completely whole?

Do not listen to the finite wisdom of man, Beloved. Man is but man—limited by his humanity. His days are just "three score and ten." What does man know? What man does will always fall pitifully short of what God can do.

Listen to the God who said:

Call to Me, and I will...tell you great and mighty things, which you do not know. (Jeremiah 33:3)

Behold, I am the LORD, the God of all flesh; is anything too difficult for Me? (Jeremiah 32:27)

Turn to Me, and be saved, all the ends of the earth. (Isaiah 45:22)

As I say all of this, I cannot help but share with you a portion of a letter that I received from a woman who had been the victim of incest since infancy. She wrote:

In a book I am reading, the author wrote of her personal experience with incest and how much her journey with God has helped her. The only thing I took discouragingly was her analogy of an amputee—saying that's how a victim is, missing something that can never be replaced. Several days ago I saw a Christian program on abused children and they expressed the same opinion. I must admit it hit hard at first. I felt my Light, Hope, and Faith pulling away from me for a moment, till I remembered what I read in God's Word about being born again, being a new creature, about all things being past and gone.

What I got out of all this is that I'm slowly getting to be like Jesus. I have His mind. To me Jesus isn't a cripple, so I'm not. I am the only thing between God and being a whole person. I am the problem.

You may correct me if I am wrong, but I'm holding out for all of God's promises. I will not settle to learn only how to adjust, cope, and function. I'm holding on to the promise of abundant life. I believe God can heal totally. I have the faith and hope that I will arrive at that point. That's my goal—to be all Jesus says I can be and wants me to be. Without that goal, if I believed what these two sources said, I'd stop growing. I'd settle, because there is no hope if I'll always be a cripple. I said you may correct me if I'm wrong, but you needn't do that in this case because I know I'm right.

Correct her? I wouldn't dare, for according to God's Word she is right. Take a few minutes to write out a prayer to your God. Pour out your heart to Him. Are you afraid to trust in Him, to call to Him? Are you afraid that He will fail you? Tell Him. It will help. Or if you want to trust

Him, to learn to run to Him first, if you want your heart to be fully His, tell Him this. Put it in black and white. When you finish, read your prayer aloud to God. It doesn't have to be fancy or eloquent, only from your heart.

MEMORY VERSE

Behold, I am the LORD, the God of all flesh; is anything too difficult for Me?

JEREMIAH 32:27

SMALL-GROUP DISCUSSION QUESTIONS

In week one we looked at the horrible state of the people in Jeremiah's day and we talked about the state of our world, of our hurts, and of the hurts of others we know.

At the end of that lesson, we looked at Jeremiah's cry in chapter 8:21-22: "For the brokenness of the daughter of my people I am broken; I mourn, dismay has taken hold of me. Is there no balm in Gilead? Is there no physician there? Why then has not the health of the daughter of my people been restored?"

As we begin this week's lesson, let's review the verse from the book of Romans which tells us that these lessons from the Old Testament Scriptures are for us today. Romans 15:4: "For whatever was written in earlier times was written for our instruction, that through perseverance and the encouragement of the Scriptures we might have hope."

All that we learn from this study in Jeremiah and from other Old Testament passages is for *us*—right where we live today!

1. What was the root of Jeremiah's anguish, as he cried over his people?
2. How do you know there was healing available for the people over whom Jeremiah cried?

3. One of God's names clearly shows Him as the Great Physician. What is the name of God that you learned this week? What does it mean?

4. What were the events surrounding the first use of this name for God in Scripture? What was God trying to teach the people in this situation?

5. Although God wanted to heal the wounds of the people who lived in Jeremiah's time, what did the people do instead of coming to Him for their healing?

6. Briefly review the account of King Asa's life in 2 Chronicles 14–16.

   a. Describe the two events that provided him an opportunity to run to the Lord. How did he respond in each?

   b. How did God view his response each time?

   c. What insights did you gain from Asa's life that you can apply to your own life?

7. Does God heal only physical diseases? What or whom did you see Him heal in the Scriptures you looked up this week?

8. The same God who was standing ready and willing to heal Jeremiah's people stands ready and willing to heal you, your family, your friends, your nation. But is this where people run when they need healing?

   a. What are some of the places people run for help, and why do you think they run to these sources?

   b. Why do you think it is difficult for some to run to God?

9. What has this lesson meant to you?

10. The next time you are hurt or wounded, where will you run? Why?

3

THERE IS A BALM, THE WORD OF GOD

— D A Y   O N E —

T his week I want us to look at the metaphor "the balm of Gilead" and see why it became a symbol of God's healing. Don't be impatient in our study. Sometimes the pain can become so great that you wonder how you can survive if something doesn't change immediately. It may not be apparent to you yet, but God is going to use all that you are learning week by week to effect your cure. Be patient. Give God time. All that you are learning is essential for healing, so don't become weary and faint...or quit.

Now to Gilead, a territory occupied by the tribes of Gad, Reuben, and the half-tribe of Manasseh. "Geographically, Gilead proper was the hilly, wooded country north of a line from Heshbon westward to the northern end of the Dead Sea, and extending northward towards the present-day river and Wadi Yarmuk but flattening out into plains from about eighteen miles south of Yarmuk."[1] In this region a balm was produced which was known not only for its healing properties but also for its cosmetic benefits.

The combination of healing and cosmetic properties in one balm is interesting. Stop and think about it for a moment. Don't you know people who have experienced healing and who, as a result, have become more beautiful? Once the bitterness, resentment, anxiety, or pain is removed, there comes a new softness, a quiet serenity bringing new beauty.

I want to keep taking you back to the Word of God because it is an important part of the healing process. More than that, it's crucial! As you look up the following verses, note what you learn that pertains to the balm or note where the balm comes from.

1. Genesis 37:25

2. Jeremiah 46:11

Gilead would apply to either the whole or a part of the Transjordanian lands occupied by the tribes I have just mentioned. However, Gilead was not only known for the balm it produced. It was also known as a place where people fled when they were in trouble. Jacob fled there from Laban, his father-in-law (Genesis 31:21-55). The Israelites fled there when being pursued by the Philistines (1 Samuel 13:7). And David fled there when being pursued by Absalom (2 Samuel 17:22-29). Under Moses, it was declared a city of refuge.

3. Look up Joshua 20:1-9 and record what you learn about the purpose of a city of refuge. Write down the name of the city in Gilead that served as a city of refuge.

O Beloved, as a child of God, where do you run in the time of trouble? What is your city of refuge? Where is your Gilead?

— D A Y   T W O —

Yesterday I asked you where you ran in the time of trouble, in the hour of need. I asked you what or who your refuge has been in times past. So often we have a tendency to turn to the "arm of flesh" instead of to our God. We can be quick to run to counselors, psychologists, psychiatrists, or to the reasoning of man, and in the process we can miss what God has for us.

Where would God have you run in the time of trouble or need?

Remember when we examined Jeremiah 8? Jeremiah was dismayed because the people's wounds were curable but they were not accepting God's cure. They listened to every prophet who came down the road proclaiming his dreams and visions, but they would not listen to God nor pay attention to His Word, the balm of Gilead.

I remember the evening when I went to Him in prayer after reading this passage in Jeremiah 8. I was in Dallas, Texas, and it was a Saturday night. A friend had settled me into one of her guest bedrooms, brought me a hot cup of tea, and left me to be alone with the Lord. I needed the quiet. I was desperate for time with my Father—to hear His voice, to learn from Him. As I poured out my need to Him in prayer, He laid Jeremiah on my heart. From there, using my concordance, God took me to Psalm 107. There I found a verse which paralleled God's use of the metaphor "the balm of Gilead." And with that scripture came insight after insight of how the balm of Gilead can be used to heal the brokenness of His people. On that day, God gave me the seedbed of this book.

Oh, what God has done since then as He has allowed me to teach these truths to others around the country! Truly, I have seen our Father heal wounds that man thought could never be healed. But then, isn't that just like the God of the impossible—the One who said, "Call to Me, and

I will answer you, and I will tell you great and mighty things, which you do not know" (Jeremiah 33:3)?

Read through Psalm 107.

1. Color or mark in a distinctive way every recurrence of the repeated phrase "Then they cried to the LORD in their trouble; He delivered them out of their distresses."* (Each phrase need not be worded exactly the same, but must say in essence the same thing.)

2. There is another key, repeated phrase in this psalm. Find it, and in a distinctive way mark it so that it will be set apart from the phrase you have already marked.

3. Now list the various distresses God's people faced as related in this psalm.

4. What verse in Psalm 107 shows you that healing comes from the Word of God? Write out that verse.

* See page 271 for section on marking your Bible.

Over and over again the psalmist describes the varied states of distress in which God's people found themselves. As you read, the tension builds, relieved only by the words "Then they cried out to the LORD in their trouble; He saved them out of their distresses" (Psalm 107:13).

Twice we read this phrase, and then we come to verse 17: "Fools, because of their rebellious way, and because of their iniquities, were afflicted. Their soul abhorred all kinds of food; and they drew near to the gates of death. Then they cried out to the LORD in their trouble; He saved them out of their distresses. HE SENT HIS WORD AND HEALED THEM, AND DELIVERED THEM FROM THEIR DESTRUCTIONS" (Psalm 107:17-20, caps mine).

There it is! The Word of God that can heal the soul. You—anyone— can be delivered from your pit of despair because there is a balm of Gilead, and there is a Great Physician there!

I pray you will wrap yourself tightly in the security blanket of this truth. At first glance you may think what I am saying is simplistic. You may be tempted to reject it or to think I'm naive. I understand.

However, I believe that if you will hear me out, God might use what I want to say to transform your life as He has mine.

– D A Y   T H R E E –

In John 6:63 Jesus made the statement that the words which He spoke "are spirit and are life." Unlike man's words, God's Word is life-giving because it is literally the Word of God. God's Word didn't originate with man. "No prophecy of Scripture is a matter of one's own interpretation, for no prophecy was ever made by an act of human will" (2 Peter 1:20-21). When you read the Word of God, you are not looking at man's analysis of God, Satan, man, creation, history, salvation, life, death, the future, etc. The Bible is God's book, given to us through men who as they were "moved by the Holy Spirit spoke from God" (2 Peter 1:21).

In 2 Timothy 3:16 we read: "All Scripture is inspired by God." The

Greek word for *inspired* is *theopneustos*. This is the only time it's used in the New Testament. *Theopneustos* means "God-breathed." Thus, the Word of God is unique. It is the only book that is supernatural, divine in its origin. That's why it is living—its words originated with God. Therefore, God's words are exactly what Jesus said they were—spirit and life. No wonder it can heal!

1. Read 2 Timothy 3:16-17, and then list the things for which the Word of God is profitable.

   a.

   b.

   c.

   d.

2. According to 2 Timothy 3:17, what is accomplished by the Word of God?

— D A Y   F O U R —

Since the Word of God is God-breathed, it is profitable for doctrine. Doctrine is what people believe, what they adhere to, the creed or truth by which they live.

If you or I want to know what is right and what is wrong, what is truth and what is a lie, then we need to know what the Word of God has to say about it, either in specific words or in principle or precept. Jesus prayed to the Father, asking that He would sanctify us in truth, and then He made this statement, "Thy word is truth" (John 17:17).

Anytime you come across something that is contrary or contradictory to the Word of God, you can know immediately that you do not have the truth. Whoever wrote it, said it, or taught it was wrong. You are deceived if you believe something that is contrary to the Word of God or that in principle or precept contradicts the Bible. If you embrace anything that contradicts or is contrary to God's Word, you have chosen to believe man above God. You have made the wrong choice! It doesn't matter what it has done for you or for others, nor does it matter what supposed proof you have that the Word of God is wrong. I must tell you, you are simply deceived. Either God's Word is what God says it is, or it is all a lie.

The Bible is the only book which, in its entirety, is composed of the very words of life, the very precepts of God. And if you are ever going to be healed, if you are ever going to be whole, then you must have the balm of Gilead, the Word of God.

Not only is God's Word truth—the doctrine or teaching by which we are to live—it's also profitable for *reproof.* The Bible reproves us because it shows us where we are wrong, where we are off track.

God's Word is our plumb line by which we are to measure everything we hear, everything we believe, everything by which we live. In case you don't know what a plumb line is, let me describe one. A plumb line is a string with a plumb bob at the end of it that gives the line weight, causing the line to fall in a straight line. If you were hanging wallpaper and you wanted to make sure it was straight, you would drop a plumb line. To check the straightness of a door, for example, a carpenter hangs a plumb line. When the plumb line stops swinging, the carpenter checks the straightness of the door by following the line of the plumb line rather than following the line of the door. Although the door might look straight, if it doesn't match the plumb line, he knows it is off.

How does this apply to healing our hurts? Someone may tell you that if you are hurting, you ought to do "such and such."

They might tell you that if you were hurt by your parents and are feeling suppressed anger, you need to get alone, pretend a pillow is your parent, and take out your frustrations on it.

They might say that if you feel rejected, you need to go back to the womb, and relive everything you remember from that point on.

However, the Word of God is your plumb line, so if the counsel you are receiving does not agree with it, either in specific teaching or in principle, then the counsel is not accurate. Your counselors may be lovely people, well liked and well thought of. They may have impressive degrees and professional training. They may have helped others. But their counsel is not from God if it in any way is not in accord with God's Word.

It is vital that you know God's Word and that you allow it to dwell in you richly. We need to know the Word of God so that it can keep us from ungodly counsel which would lead us into ungodly reasoning and unbiblical behavior.

Let me close today with one question: What priority does the Bible have in your life, Beloved? Have you given yourself to a diligent study of its precepts?

— D A Y   F I V E —

According to 2 Timothy 3:16, God's Word is not only profitable for doctrine and reproof but also for correction. It is often in the area of correction that the healing process takes place. Correction is knowing how to take what is wrong and make it right. So often when people are wounded by someone else, they harbor hurt and bitterness, nursing it rather than releasing it.

They don't know bitterness and unforgiveness will keep them from being healed. How often I have seen people in this situation! And, bless their hearts, they don't know how to let go of their bitterness. They wonder how they can ever forgive.

God's Word is so thorough that it not only gives us truth and shows us where we are wrong, it also shows us how to take what is wrong and make it right.

And that is what you are going to learn to do in this book. And do you know what? If you will do what God says, it will work. You *can* be healed. When I say *healed*, I don't mean you'll never experience pain again. Nor do I mean that the past will never again rear its ugly head. I mean you will be able to deal with your hurt in such a way that you will "live as more than a conqueror." You will have God's answer on how to deal with your hurt so that it doesn't harm you but works together for your good.

You have God as your Great Physician, and you have the Word of God which heals. All you need is faith to obey. If you don't have that kind of faith, you can pray, "God, I believe. Help, Thou, my unbelief," and He will.

According to 2 Timothy 3:16, the Word of God is also profitable for training in righteousness. To live righteously is simply to live according to the Word of God. And this, once again, is where healing begins—in doing what God says to do, no matter how you feel, no matter what you think. This is faith, "and without faith it is impossible to please Him, for he who comes to God must believe that He is, and that He is a rewarder of those who seek Him" (Hebrews 11:6). You cannot out trust God!

I will never forget a woman who came to me years ago, distraught because her husband was having an affair. It had so thrown her that she began seeing a psychiatrist who told her that it would take two years of counseling before she would ever be healed. I remember sitting with her in the home where I taught a weekly Bible class. Perched on the end of the bed in a guest bedroom, I looked at that face, at her long, dark brown hair, and her beautiful but sad eyes, and I wondered how any man could walk away from someone who was so in love with him. After I had listened, praying all the time for wisdom, I found myself reaching over and taking both of her hands in mine and saying, "Darling, you can be healed today if you will only believe and obey God."

I don't usually tell people they can be healed "today," for often healing is a process. But I do say, "You can be healed if you will only believe and obey God." We'll talk about that more in just a minute, but let me go back to my friend.

She was healed that day. That healing has lasted all of these years, even carrying her through more trials. When my friend told me she wanted to be healed, I shared God's Word as it related to her situation. When I finished, we slipped down onto the soft, blue carpet. The warm sun fell on our backs like a touch from the Father as we knelt and called out to our Jehovah-rapha. He heard. There we embraced one another, wiped our eyes, and got up from our knees. It was all right now. Whatever happened, she knew God was in control. My new friend was going to do what God said.

She went home, called her psychiatrist, and told him that she didn't need him anymore. And she didn't. I knew that for sure when she came to me several weeks later after our Wednesday Bible class and said, "Kay, I want you to pray for me. I don't love that woman like I should." What I saw in my friend was a desire to be like Jesus—there is nothing healthier or more healing than that! She was willing to deal with this adulterous woman as Jesus did—in love.

His name is Jehovah-rapha, the God who heals. He is the Physician in Gilead, and you can cry, "Heal me, O LORD, and I will be healed; save me and I will be saved" (Jeremiah 17:14). He will heal; He will save. I know—I have seen it in my own life, and I have seen it again and again in the lives of others. His Word is true. His name is a strong tower; the righteous run into it and are safe (Proverbs 18:10).

– D A Y   S I X –

There is one more truth we need to see in 2 Timothy 3:17. The reason the Word of God is profitable for doctrine, reproof, correction and instruction in righteousness is so that you and I "may be adequate, equipped for every good work." Marvin Vincent, a Greek scholar of renown, says that the idea of complete or adequate is "that of mutual, symmetrical adjustment of all that goes to make the man: harmonious combination of different qualities and powers."[2]

Do you see what God is saying? The Word of God can "adjust" us in all our parts. Let me go on, and then I will put it all together. The English transliteration for the Greek word for *adequate* is *artios,* which means "perfect or complete." This word and the Greek word for *equipped* are a play on words. *Equipped* is *exartizō* and means "to equip fully, to accomplish, to thoroughly furnish." God is saying that the Word of God is ultimately all you and I need in order to be what we need to be.

The Word of God has the practical answers for all of life's needs. It will thoroughly furnish you for every good work of life. Vincent, in commenting on the words, "unto all good works" or "for every good work," says, "It is to be noted that the test of the divine inspiration of Scripture is here placed in its practical usefulness."[3]

Now can you see why God's Word can heal you? It is because His Word is different than man's. God's Word is truth. It is alive. It can heal if you will accept it in faith and walk accordingly.

If God is able to save man from himself and his sin, if God is able to save man from hell, and if God is able to make a person a new creature in Christ Jesus all through faith in His Word alone, then can't God enable us to live above our hurts as we take Him at His word?

May God send His Word and heal you and deliver you out of all your destructions. In Psalm 107:20 destructions can also be translated "pits"! If life is the pits, the Word can get you out!

Write out and memorize 2 Timothy 3:16-17.

— D A Y   S E V E N —

For the child of God all things work together for good. This truth is reality because God is the Great Redeemer. He redeems all your past and uses it to conform you into the image of His Son. He is for you, not against you. And if He is for you, who can be against you? Neither death, nor life, nor angels, nor principalities, nor things present, nor things to come, nor powers, nor height, nor depth, nor any other created thing, shall be able to separate you from the love of God, which is in Christ Jesus our Lord (Romans 8:28-39, selected verses).

God's love is an unconditional, everlasting, transforming love. A love demonstrated and received at Calvary. And it is at Calvary that you, Beloved of God, will find your Gilead—your city of refuge, your place of healing.

When Jeremiah asked if there was a balm in Gilead and a physician there, he expected a response of yes. He had asked this question because he wanted his people to remember that God was the only one who could satisfy all of their needs, heal all of their wounds, and provide them with everything they needed for life and godliness.

As you saw in your first week of study, God's people had committed two evils in Jeremiah's day. First, they had forsaken God, the fountain of living waters. Second, they had hewn for themselves cisterns, broken cisterns, which couldn't hold water (Jeremiah 2:13). In other words, they had turned from God and His ways to the flesh and its ways. They did not draw from Him that which is essential for life—living water.

How like our "Americanized" Christianity! We have needed healing, but instead of running to our Father and asking Him what to do, we have turned to man's psychology, to man's philosophy, to our humanistic version of Christianity, or to our own understanding. Like the Israelites of old, we have turned from the wellspring of all of God's sufficiency to the cistern of man's reasoning.

A cistern is simply a place to store something, usually water. What you put into a cistern is what you get out of it. In contrast, a wellspring has an unseen source from which you draw. The people of Jeremiah's day had forsaken the fountain of living waters for broken cisterns which couldn't even hold water! We do the same thing when we turn from the Word of God to the counsel and wisdom of man for healing our hurts.

Beloved, I don't know how this book got into your hands, but I do know that God, in His sovereignty, put it there. He has a way to heal your hurts or the hurts of those whom you love.

You can be healed if you will be healed His way. You can be healed if you will run to Calvary, your city of refuge.

Remember, there is a balm in Gilead and there is a Physician there. You can cry, "Heal me, O Lord, and I will be healed!" We are going to learn how in the weeks to come.

MEMORY VERSE

All Scripture is inspired by God and profitable for teaching, for reproof, for correction, for training in righteousness.

2 TIMOTHY 3:16

SMALL-GROUP DISCUSSION QUESTIONS

In week two we saw that one of God's names is Jehovah-rapha and that His desire is to have us run to Him in times of distress so that He can heal and restore us—not only physically but in every area of our lives.

In that lesson we looked at the first use of the name Jehovah-rapha and in that account saw that God's design was for His people to come to Him in time of need. We also studied the life of King Asa and how God was grieved over Asa's failure to turn to Him first when he needed healing.

1. When we looked at Jeremiah's cry in 8:22, we saw that he asked whether or not there were two things in Gilead. One of these was a Great Physician, which we learned was God. What was the second thing that the people needed for their restoration?

2. As you read Psalm 107, what did you see that God would use to bring their healing?

3. From your study in Psalm 107, what did you see that paralleled the metaphor "the balm of Gilead?
   This week you studied a city called Gilead. What two things was Gilead known for?

4. From your study in 2 Timothy 3:16-17 on the Word of God...
   a. what is the Word of God profitable for?
   b. what is accomplished by the Word of God?

5. Briefly discuss what each of the following means:
   a. Doctrine
   b. Reproof
   c. Correction
   d. Instruction in righteousness

6. What does it mean to be "adequate, equipped for every good work"?

7. How is God's Word different from the words of man?
   Do you see any parallels between what you learned about the Word of God and the two things for which Gilead was known?

8. In light of your study this week, do you believe that God's Word has the answers for the hurts of your family, friends,...for your hurts? Why or why not?

9. If all that we have talked about this week is true, and the Word of God is profitable for doctrine, reproof, correction, and instruction in righteousness that the man or woman of God may be equipped for every good work, then what should your attitude be toward the Word of God?

10. What has this week's lesson meant to you personally? What will you change in your life as a result of this lesson?

4

CALVARY'S LOVE...
IT'S HELL, IT'S HEALING

From the moment she knew she had conceived, she had loved her son. Now, as an adult, he had suddenly thrown up a wall between them. No longer would he take her in his arms. No longer would he come to her home. A wall was there, a wall so impenetrable it could not be bulldozed down.

The pain was enormous. She could think of nothing else. He felt she had failed him as a mother. And she had. She hadn't meant to...but was it as bad as he thought it was? Was it an incurable failure? One that would cripple him and their relationship forever?

The pain was excruciating. All of her life her goal had been to be a good mother and a good wife. She had missed her goal as a mother. She would not get another chance. The thought devastated her. She began to relive her past, analyzing what she could have done differently. Her despair increased. She could not undo the past. She had wanted nothing more than to have her children and husband rise up and call her blessed, nothing more than to hear her Lord say, "Well done, my good and faithful servant."

My heart ached for her. I could understand the longing of her heart. I, too, loved my sons. I, too, had wanted what she wanted.

She told me that her pain reminded her of how she had heard heart attacks described—dull, heavy, never ceasing. She felt as if she had a boulder on her chest. Her heart had been raped, deprived of her son's love. The pain immobilized her...until she ran in prayer to her Father God, her Jehovah-rapha.

Then God reminded her that He understood. He understood her desire for intimacy with her son. Some of His children had cut Him off, had ceased to spend time with Him. They felt He had failed them. "But, Father, You didn't fail," she almost yelled at Him. "I did."

And then, in answer to her anguish, that still, small voice came into her mind, "I know I did not fail, and I know that you were not perfect. But remember, I am greater than your failures. I am God, and I have promised you—and your son, whether he believes it or not—that all things will work together for good.

"He is mine, and I will use it all to conform him into the image of my Son. Now, what are my promises? Believe them. Live by them. Do what I have taught you to do. Regardless of how your son responds, believe and obey me. You cannot redeem the past. I can. Walk in faith. Either my Word is true, or it isn't. And you know it is truth."

As my friend began to wrestle with whether her thoughts were simply what she wanted to hear or if they were from the Holy Spirit, she told me with a chagrined look that she finally gave in. She knew that what had been in her heart was in accord with the Word of God and the character of God. The wrestling was over. Faith pinned her to the mat.

How I rejoiced! Although her situation didn't change for a long, long time, she was no longer incapacitated by her sorrow. She found her refuge, her Gilead, and there she dwells by faith.

This week I want us to look at what I will call the Christian's Gilead—a place of refuge where any child of God can run and cry out, "Heal me, O LORD, and I will be healed; save me and I will be saved, for Thou art my praise" (Jeremiah 17:14).

– D A Y   T W O –

Where is the Christian's city of refuge? Where can we turn? Where will we find all that we need?

The cross of Calvary. There we receive all God wrought for us through our Lord's death and resurrection. At the cross we meet Jesus as our Jehovah-rapha, the Lord who heals. At the cross we meet Jesus as the One who has experienced the pain and hell which we have endured.

Because of the cross, you and I have a representative in heaven who can intercede on our behalf. At the cross Jesus fully experienced the ravages of sin, pain, and suffering. You haven't lived through anything that Jesus has not also endured. He was made sin for you. That is Calvary love...the hell, the healing. Your refuge is Calvary's cross, Beloved. There is no wound that Calvary cannot heal.

Let me show you why I say that our Gilead is Calvary's cross. Remember we saw that the word *rapha* means "to mend, to cure, to repair thoroughly, to make whole." The word rapha is used in Isaiah 53:5.

Look up Isaiah 53:5, and write it out in the space provided.

Isaiah 53 clearly points to the person of Jesus Christ. Many Jewish people ignore a study of this chapter because they find it hard to explain away. It clearly points to one person bearing their iniquities.

The prophecy of Isaiah 53 begins at Isaiah 52:13. Your assignment for today will be an incredible blessing. Read from Isaiah 52:13 to Isaiah 53:12 aloud. As you read, each time you come to a personal pronoun such as "our" or "us," substitute your name.

When you finish reading the chapter, and substituting your name for the personal pronouns, write out the prayer that is on your heart in the light of this chapter.

▶ ISAIAH 52:13–53:12

13 Behold, My servant will prosper, He will be high and lifted up, and greatly exalted.

14 Just as many were astonished at you, My people, so His appearance was marred more than any man, and His form more than the sons of men.

15 Thus He will sprinkle many nations, kings will shut their mouths on account of Him; for what had not been told them they will see, and what they had not heard they will understand.

1 Who has believed our message? And to whom has the arm of the LORD been revealed?

2 For He grew up before Him like a tender shoot, and like a root out of parched ground; He has no stately form or majesty that we should look upon Him, nor appearance that we should be attracted to Him.

3 He was despised and forsaken of men, a man of sorrows, and acquainted with grief; and like one from whom men hide their face, He was despised, and we did not esteem Him.

4 Surely our griefs He Himself bore, and our sorrows He carried; yet we ourselves esteemed Him stricken, smitten of God, and afflicted.

5 But He was pierced through for our transgressions, He was crushed for our iniquities; the chastening for our well-being fell upon Him, and by His scourging we are healed.

6 All of us like sheep have gone astray, each of us has turned to his own way; but the LORD has caused the iniquity of us all to fall on Him.

7 He was oppressed and He was afflicted, yet He did not open His mouth; like a lamb that is led to slaughter, and like a sheep that is silent before its shearers, so He did not open His mouth.

8 By oppression and judgment He was taken away; and as for His generation, who considered that He was cut off out of the land of the living, for the transgression of my people to whom the stroke was due?

⁹ His grave was assigned with wicked men, yet He was with a rich man in His death, because He had done no violence, nor was there any deceit in His mouth.

¹⁰ But the LORD was pleased to crush Him, putting Him to grief; if He would render Himself as a guilt offering, He will see His offspring, He will prolong His days, and the good pleasure of the LORD will prosper in His hand.

¹¹ As a result of the anguish of His soul, He will see it and be satisfied; by His knowledge the Righteous One, My Servant, will justify the many, as He will bear their iniquities.

¹² Therefore, I will allot Him a portion with the great, and He will divide the booty with the strong; because He poured out Himself to death, and was numbered with the transgressors; yet He Himself bore the sin of many, and interceded for the transgressors.

Write out the prayer that is on your heart as a result of this chapter.

— D A Y   T H R E E —

Jesus not only healed through His life, He healed through His death, and He heals through His present ministry of intercession. Before we move on in our study, I want you to see and understand how Jesus accomplishes our healing through these three means.

You may be wondering when we are going to get to the specifics of how to handle wounds that have come from various sorts of abuse—emotional, physical, sexual; from failures of the past; from words that have left seemingly permanent scars; from rejection, etc. Don't despair!

We will see how each of these can be healed. However, all healing finds its basis at the cross of Calvary. Through Calvary you have access to your Great Physician, Jesus. He alone is God, and He is the God who heals all of our hurts. So it is on Calvary that we must focus our attention for a few days.

Now, let's go to Isaiah 53:4 where we see how Jesus healed through His life. In Isaiah 53:4 we read, "Surely our griefs (pains) He Himself bore, and our sorrows (sickness) He carried."

The best interpreter of Scripture is Scripture. One verse's explanation of another is the interpretation to which we must adhere. In Matthew 8:17 we find an explanation of Isaiah 53:4.

As you will see, Matthew 8:5-17 tells of Jesus' ministry in Capernaum. Capernaum, where the apostle Peter resided, was predominantly a Gentile city. As you read through this passage, answer the following questions:

1. What is Jesus doing in Capernaum? What is the focus of His ministry in this account?

2. Explain how Isaiah 53:4 relates to this passage.

3. According to what you have learned, when was Isaiah 53:4 fulfilled and how?

MATTHEW 8:5-17

5 And when He had entered Capernaum, a centurion came to Him, entreating Him,

6 and saying, "Lord, my servant is lying paralyzed at home, suffering great pain."

7 And He said to him, "I will come and heal him."

8 But the centurion answered and said, "Lord, I am not worthy for You to come under my roof, but just say the word, and my servant will be healed.

9 "For I, too, am a man under authority, with soldiers under me; and I say to this one, 'Go!' and he goes, and to another, 'Come!' and he comes, and to my slave, 'Do this!' and he does it."

10 Now when Jesus heard this, He marveled, and said to those who were following, "Truly I say to you, I have not found such great faith with anyone in Israel.

11 "And I say to you, that many shall come from east and west, and recline at the table with Abraham, and Isaac, and Jacob, in the kingdom of heaven;

12 "but the sons of the kingdom shall be cast out into the outer darkness; in that place there shall be weeping and gnashing of teeth."

13 And Jesus said to the centurion, "Go your way; let it be done to you as you have believed." And the servant was healed that very hour.

14 And when Jesus had come to Peter's home, He saw his mother-in-law lying sick in bed with a fever.

15 And He touched her hand, and the fever left her; and she arose, and waited on Him.

16 And when evening had come, they brought to Him many who were demon-possessed; and He cast out the spirits with a word, and healed all who were ill

¹⁷ in order that what was spoken through Isaiah the prophet might be fulfilled, saying, "HE HIMSELF TOOK OUR INFIRMITIES, AND CARRIED AWAY OUR DISEASES."

Tomorrow we will look at Isaiah 53:5-6 and how Jesus healed through His death. There is so much to be learned, and it will prove so incredibly beneficial to your daily living. I can't wait to share it all with you, my friend. There is hope, so don't despair either for yourself or for your loved ones.

− D A Y   F O U R −

As I said earlier, all wounds ultimately have their root in sin. We have wounded others, or they us. Either way, it has been because of sin. We chose (or others chose) to walk independently of God and His Word. We chose not to listen, to believe, or to obey God.

Sin wounds. Sin mars. Sin disfigures. Sin destroys. And were it not for the cross of Calvary, sin's destruction would be permanent, irreversible. But God! How I love those words, "But God."

In Isaiah 53:5 we read, "But He [Jesus, God the Son] was pierced through for our transgressions, He was crushed for our iniquities; the chastening for our well-being fell upon Him, and by His scourging we are healed."

Healed! Healed of what?

Once again, Scripture must interpret Scripture. Therefore, write out 1 Peter 2:24-25. As you do, read the verses aloud. It will help you memorize what you read.

Before we discuss these verses, one more question: What parallel, if any, do you see between Isaiah 53:6 and 1 Peter 2:25?

According to Isaiah 53:5-6 and 1 Peter 2:24-25, the cross was God's means of healing you of your sin so that you could live a righteous life. Sin wounds; the cross heals. The cross heals because it deals with sin. Through the healing power of Calvary, you can live a righteous life.

To live righteously is to live according to what God says is right. No matter what has happened to you, you can live without bitterness or hatred. You can live a life free from that which would otherwise distort, disfigure, or destroy you. Bitterness can go, and forgiveness can be received and extended. You can be whole! You can be healed! Next week we will study why all of this is possible.

Beloved, do you feel that you can never let go of bitterness? Do you feel that you can never forgive those who've wounded you? That bitterness will be your lifelong companion? I understand your feelings.

However, I urge you to rest in what you are learning. Take it one day at a time. Keep praying, "Heal me, O Lord, and I will be healed; save me and I will be saved, for Thou art my praise."

Is there any bitterness or unforgiveness in your heart? Whom is it against and why? Write out your thoughts. You need not be too specific if it is too hard.

I want you to finish today's study by reading Psalm 22. Jesus not only paid for your sin, He became sin for you. What did all of this cost Him? Psalm 22 gives us a detailed description of what happens when a person is crucified. Read it prayerfully and thoughtfully.[1]

Now, as you consider all you have learned this week, list what you think Jesus experienced on the cross when He was made sin for you.

− D A Y   F I V E −

If you are going to learn to deal with your hurts God's way, you must know Jesus as your refuge.

At the beginning of this week's study, I said that the Christian's Gilead is Calvary. Healing comes from Jehovah-rapha—from our God, our Savior, our Lord.

When Jesus was on earth, He healed the sick and the demon-possessed through His life. When He went to Calvary, He healed us of our sins through His death. Before we move on, let's take another look at this truth from the perspective of Colossians 2:6-15. Keep in mind what we studied yesterday.

1. Read the following passage carefully, marking each reference to *you*. You might color it or put a little stick figure like this—y♀u—over each occurence of the word. When you finish, at the end of the text list everything you learned from this passage about "you."

2. Read through this passage again, and mark every use of any of these three phrases: *in Him*, or *through Him*, or *with Him*. Use a different color, or draw a diagram like this ⟨⟨ in him ⟩⟩ over the phrase. When you finish, list all that occurred in, through, or with Him, as you listed all that you learned regarding "you."

▶ COLOSSIANS 2:6-15

6 As you therefore have received Christ Jesus the Lord, so walk in Him,

7 having been firmly rooted and now being built up in Him and established in your faith, just as you were instructed, and overflowing with gratitude.

8 See to it that no one takes you captive through philosophy and empty deception, according to the tradition of men, according to the elementary principles of the world, rather than according to Christ.

9 For in Him all the fulness of Deity dwells in bodily form,

10 and in Him you have been made complete, and He is the head over all rule and authority;

11 and in Him you were also circumcised with a circumcision made without hands, in the removal of the body of the flesh by the circumcision of Christ;

12 having been buried with Him in baptism, in which you were also raised up with Him through faith in the working of God, who raised Him from the dead.

13 And when you were dead in your transgressions and the uncircumci-

sion of your flesh, He made you alive together with Him, having forgiven us

all our transgressions,

14 having canceled out the certificate of debt consisting of decrees against

us and which was hostile to us; and He has taken it out of the way, having

nailed it to the cross.

15 When He had disarmed the rulers and authorities, He made a public

display of them, having triumphed over them through Him.

WHAT I LEARNED ABOUT ME   WHAT OCCURRED IN,
                                 THROUGH, OR WITH HIM

3. How does what you have observed in Colossians 2:6-15 relate to what we have been studying this week? How has this passage spoken to you?

– D A Y   S I X –

So far we have studied how Jesus healed through His life and His death. Today we'll look at His third means of healing: intercession.

Do you know what Jesus is doing right now? The answer to this question was powerfully brought home to me when we piloted our Precept Bible study course on Hebrews. Before we ever release a Precept or In & Out Study to the public, we first work through it with our faithful students here in Chattanooga.

I will never forget what Emily Farmer told me. At the time she was the executive producer of our radio program, "How Can I Live." When she gets excited about something, she has an impish smile, and her brown eyes sparkle with joy. As I looked at her, I knew something good was coming.

"Kay, do you know what I saw as I studied Hebrews?" Without pausing, she continued, "Jesus' work as far as our salvation is complete. When He hung on the cross, He said, 'It is finished.' Therefore, according to Hebrews, His ministry on our behalf is simply to continually intercede for us! That is what He lives to do for us now! Isn't that wonderful?"

It was wonderful—awesome, really. The more I have thought about what Emily shared, the more it has ministered to me. I have gone to teach and thought, *Right now, Jesus is interceding for me.*

I have been witnessing and felt at a loss as to what to say next, and I have thought, *Jesus is making intercession for me.*

I have found myself in difficult situations and breathed a sigh of relief because I remembered, *Jesus is interceding—that's what He lives for now.*

I've hurt, and I've known that I could go on. Jesus understands—and He's interceding.

And I know the Father hears and answers His prayers.

What a divine and incomprehensible mystery! What a marvelous reality to live, moment by moment! I pray that I will always remember this truth. I am never alone in any situation—never left to my own wisdom, prowess, ability, or endurance. Jesus is interceding! Because of that, there is no situation out from under His knowledge, control, or purpose. My circumstances may be hard, difficult, but "He is able to save forever those who draw near to God through Him, since He always lives to make intercession for them" (Hebrews 7:25).

O Father, teach me to continually draw near.

Write out and memorize Hebrews 7:24-25.

Beloved, are you hurting? Remember:

Since then we have a great high priest who has passed through the heavens, Jesus the Son of God, let us hold fast our confession. For we do not have a high priest who cannot sympathize with our weaknesses, but one who has been tempted in all things as we are, yet without sin. Let us therefore draw near with confidence to the throne of grace, that we may receive mercy and may find grace to help in time of need. (Hebrews 4:14-16)

What a refuge we have in Jesus, our Lord who heals!

— D A Y   S E V E N —

Many of us, although saved by faith, live as if faith is not enough for our daily living. We slip back into a mentality of "I've got to do my part to please God" or "I can't simply trust the Bible. I need more than just the Word of God in order to live my life successfully."

This type of thinking leads many to believe they need something instead of, or in addition to, God's Word if they are ever to be healed.

But regarding thinking like this, I must ask, What does the Word of God say? What does it teach? Is 2 Timothy 3:16-17 true? Is the Bible sufficient so that the child of God might be perfect, thoroughly furnished unto every good work? Does the Bible provide us with the answers so that the child of God can adequately handle anything that life brings into his or her existence? The only correct answer to these questions is yes—a resounding yes!

My friend, what is your concept of the Bible? Do you believe it is as it claims to be: the very Word of God, God-breathed, without error, and the very bread by which the child of God is to live? Or do you believe it is filled with myths, stories passed down around campfires from generation to generation until they were finally recorded in an exaggerated way in a book said to be the Word of God? Do you believe the Bible merely contains

God's words and that these can be sorted out and declared to be His words or not His words by theological scholars? Or do you believe the Bible to be only God's Word as it personally speaks or relates to you in a spiritual sense?

What do you believe about the Word of God? Write it out.

Now look up the following verses to see what God says regarding His Word, the Bible. Write out each verse or the essence of what the verse says. I will leave out 2 Timothy 3:16-17 since we have covered it. But don't forget what it says!

1. 2 Peter 1:20-21

2. Luke 24:25-27

3. Isaiah 8:20

4. John 17:17

5. John 6:63

Whose word are you going to accept regarding the Word of God—man's or God's?

MEMORY VERSE

But He, on the other hand, because He abides forever, holds His priesthood permanently. Hence, also, He is able to save forever those who draw near to God through Him, since He always lives to make intercession for them.

HEBREWS 7:24-25

SMALL-GROUP DISCUSSION QUESTIONS

In week three we looked at the balm of Gilead, and we saw that this phrase was a metaphor used in Psalm 107 for the Word of God.

We looked at 2 Timothy 3:16 and learned what the Word of God was profitable for and what is accomplished by it.

We saw that the distressed in Psalm 107 cried out to God and that

He sent His Word and healed them. We saw that healing comes through knowing and applying the Word of God to our situations of life.

We discovered that the Word of God was the plumb line by which we could measure everything.

Because of all that we learned last week, the logical conclusion to draw was that in order to live godly lives we must know the Word so that we have a standard by which we can measure every situation of life.

1. Where is the place of refuge for a Christian? Why?

2. This week you studied the different ways by which Jesus provided for your healing. What were these three ways?

3. All of us hurt—or have hurt—in some way. What really is the root of any wound that you or I have suffered?

4. There was a wonderful provision made for the healing of the root of our wounds. Where was this provision made? Where does our healing find its basis?

5. In Isaiah 53:4 we read that "surely our griefs He Himself bore, and our sorrows He carried." According to what you read in Matthew 8, when was the scripture in Isaiah 53:4 fulfilled?

6. How does Jesus' work on Calvary provide for our healing?

7. What is the means by which Jesus keeps providing for our healing? (Hint: Even as you are reading this, He is making provision for your healing in this way!)

8. What is the precious truth that Hebrews 4:14-16 reveals about Jesus, your High Priest? Does He understand you as He intercedes on your behalf?

9. Do you think that Jesus can truly sympathize with your situations? Think back through what you have studied this week and think of the different things Jesus suffered for your salvation and healing.

10. In the light of last week's lesson and what Christ did to make a way for you to be healed, what are you going to do with your hurts? What are you going to share with others who are hurting and who think that they will be crippled by their hurts for the rest of their lives?

ARE YOU FREE TO CHOOSE?

— DAY ONE —

O ne cannot speak of the Crucifixion apart from the Resurrection. The bodily resurrection of our Lord is an essential ingredient of the gospel. Without it, we would still be "dead in our trespasses and sins." If the dead are not raised, we are without hope. It is the Resurrection that gives us newness of life.

This truth is clearly seen in Romans 6. However, before we begin our study I want to make sure you understand the significance of the Resurrection and exactly how one is saved.

Christ's resurrection testifies to two vital truths. One, it shows that God was propitiated, or satisfied, with the substitutionary death of Christ. Jesus became the bearer of our sins. In Romans 4:25 we read, "He who was delivered up because of our transgressions, and was raised because of our justification." "Raised because of our justification" means that because Jesus' payment for our sins was adequate, God could declare us righteous, justified in His sight. Jesus was raised because His death satisfied the righteousness of our holy God.

Two, His resurrection shows us that Jesus Christ conquered death. Death had a hold over man because of his sin. However, once sin was paid for, death no longer had any holding power. "The sting of death is sin, and the power of sin is the law" (1 Corinthians 15:56). Jesus "redeemed us from the curse of the Law, having become a curse for us—for it is written,

'CURSED IS EVERYONE WHO HANGS ON A TREE'" (Galatians 3:13). His death took away the power of sin. Jesus also took the stinger out of death by paying for our sin. Therefore, because our sin is paid for in full, death has no power over us.

"Since then the children share in flesh and blood, He Himself likewise also partook of the same, that through death He might render powerless him who had the power of death, that is, the devil; and might deliver those who through fear of death were subject to slavery all their lives" (Hebrews 2:14-15). Satan can never hold a child of God in death's chains because all of his sin is covered by the blood of Jesus Christ. Therefore, resurrection is inevitable. For a Christian, death is "to be absent from the body and to be at home with the Lord" (2 Corinthians 5:8). "To live is Christ, and to die is gain" for the child of God (Philippians 1:21).

If you are a child of God, you can be absolutely sure that you never need to fear death. The moment you close your eyes in death on this earth, you will meet the lover of your soul, the healer of your wounds, the One who says you are precious in His sight.

I cannot go any further until I am sure you know exactly where you stand with God. Is He truly your heavenly Father? Have you really believed on the Lord Jesus Christ? I'm not asking to try to make you doubt a salvation that's real; I'm asking to cause you to examine yourself to see if you are in the faith. Apart from salvation you will never really know a permanent healing of your wounds. Therefore, to cry "Heal me, O Lord" without first having cried "Save me, O Lord" is futile.

Salvation belongs to the poor in spirit. Matthew 5:3 says, "Blessed are the poor in spirit, for theirs is the kingdom of heaven." If you recognize that you are spiritually destitute—totally incapable of deserving or earning salvation in any way, you are poor in spirit. Christ Jesus came into the world to save sinners (1 Timothy 1:15). The poor in spirit understand that they are sinners, totally impotent to please or to serve God.

Poverty of spirit is interwoven in the act of repentance. Repentance is a change of mind. When you repent, you see yourself as you really are and you change your mind in respect to your relationship to God the Father and to His Son, the Lord Jesus Christ. The act of repentance brings you to see sin as it is, and you come to a point where you want to be free from it.

Of course, freedom from sin comes only by believing on the Lord Jesus Christ. The one who commits sin is the slave of sin. However, if the Son shall set you free, you shall be free indeed (John 8:34,36).

The poor in spirit see their impotence to free themselves from sin. They see that freedom is possible only through Christ's substitutionary death for us. They recognize that salvation comes by grace alone.

Think on these things. Tomorrow I want to share with you how I came to salvation.

— D A Y   T W O —

Have you ever felt that you couldn't be good even if you wanted to?

Have you ever hated the things you were doing, tried to stop, but couldn't?

I understand. That's exactly the way it was for me before I was saved.

After I left Tom, I went from one man to another, searching for someone who would love me unconditionally. I didn't know God's Word said that committing sin would make me a slave to it. I wasn't saved until I was twenty-nine.

As I look back, I can see the chains that shackled me to sin. When I finally faced my immorality for what it was, I saw I could no longer excuse my behavior by society's acceptance of it. Nor could I excuse my immorality because others were immoral. What others did was not always right. My mom and dad had taught me that.

I finally saw that one day I would stand before a holy God and justly hear, "Depart from Me into everlasting fire." I hadn't been taught about the reality and certainty of hell for all of those who do not have the Son of God residing within by faith. I didn't even fear hell. I simply knew that a holy God could not condone my immorality and, therefore, could not accept me into heaven.

I determined I would quit being immoral. I would change my lifestyle. And try I did. But it didn't work. I would say, "I'm not going to do that anymore." But I would! I would go out and be immoral again. So once again, I would resolve, "I'm not going to do it anymore," but I would. Little did I realize how well I would someday relate to Paul's cry, "Wretched man that I am! Who will set me free from the body of this death?" (Romans 7:24).

I was a slave to sin. I was not poor in spirit. I thought I could set myself free. I didn't know that slaves can't free themselves. I made resolution after resolution, but resolutions couldn't unlock my chains. I felt sick. At the time I was working as a registered nurse on a research team at Johns Hopkins, and I remember thinking, *I have a sickness no one can cure! If only I were physically sick!*

When I woke up the morning of July 16, 1963, I thought, *I cannot go to work. I'm too ill—ill with a sickness that cannot be cured.* After I called the doctor I worked for and told him that I would see him on Monday, I dragged into the kitchen to bake a cake. I thought, *I'll take the boys camping.* Camping with the boys was a means to an end; I wanted them to know that I loved them, that I cared, that they were special to me. I craved being a perfect mother. But even here, I had failed. They didn't have a normal family life. Mothers shouldn't be dating; they should be living with the fathers...but I had left their father.

As I put the cake into the oven, Mark was clinging to my apron, hungry for his mommy's love. Suddenly I bent down, looked into his precious little eyes, and trembling with emotion, I stammered, "Mark, honey, Mommy has to be alone for a few minutes. Will you let me be alone just for a minute or two?"

I thought he could sense the urgency of my request as his little blond head bobbed up and down. But I had to be sure. I asked once again,

"Will you let Mommy be alone for just a few minutes?" With that, I ran out of the kitchen.

I propelled myself up the stairs by grabbing the banister and took the stairs two at a time. I had to be alone. When I entered my bedroom, I barely missed the nightstand as I collapsed on my knees. I had to get to my bed before my heart ruptured. I couldn't contain my cry any longer.

"O God, I don't care what You do to me," I sobbed as I spilled out the worst things I thought could ever happen. "I don't care if you paralyze me from the neck down. I don't care if I never see another man as long as I live. I don't care what you do to my two boys…if you will only give me peace."

That was all I prayed. There, on my knees, I received the Prince of Peace. I didn't know that this was what God called salvation. I only knew that I was clean and that Jesus was with me. Wherever I went, He would go.

In the days that followed, I knew I had been set free. My perspective on life was different. I had a hunger for the Word of God. And, wonder of wonders, I could understand it. I was no longer a slave. I had the power to say no and to live according to God's commandments. It was as if a lawkeeper had taken up residence within me.

Of course, He had! His name was the Lord Jesus Christ. I'm not saying that I didn't sin. I did. But not like I used to. Now sin was a matter of free choice, and sin was not something I casually chose! I wanted to please my God. And that I was able to do because the Godhead had taken up residence within (John 14:23).

I was healed of sin. I, who at one time had thought that God was lucky to have me on His team doing church work, had finally seen my total poverty of spirit. I was willing to deny myself, take up my cross, and follow Him. And when I finally did, I found my Gilead at the foot of the Cross.

O Beloved, have you come to the end of self?

Have you seen your total impotence, your total unworthiness? Have you seen your nothingness apart from God? And have you seen Jesus, God the Son who took upon Himself flesh and blood that He might die for you and for all mankind?

Do you believe that? Do you believe He died in your place? Do you believe that He was made sin for you, so that you, a helpless, hopeless enemy of God, might have His righteousness and His life? Have you repented—turned from self—to believe on the Lord Jesus Christ? Have you been saved from your sin? If you haven't, healing can never be yours.

Why delay? Come to Him. Call upon His name. Believe in your heart that God has raised Jesus from the dead. Confess the Lord Jesus Christ, and you will be saved, "for with the heart man believes, resulting in righteousness, and with the mouth he confesses, resulting in salvation. For the Scripture says, 'WHOEVER BELIEVES IN HIM WILL NOT BE DISAPPOINTED.'... For 'WHOEVER WILL CALL UPON THE NAME OF THE LORD WILL BE SAVED'" (Romans 10:10-11,13).

What is your response? Record it.

— D A Y   T H R E E —

There is much to see regarding your freedom from slavery to sin as a child of God.

Three of the most significant chapters in the Word of God are Romans 6, 7, and 8. Romans 6 is typed out for you. Read it through once rapidly, without stopping. Then read it again carefully and prayerfully. Read aloud.

▶ ROMANS 6

1 What shall we say then? Are we to continue in sin that grace might increase?

2 May it never be! How shall we who died to sin still live in it?

3 Or do you not know that all of us who have been baptized into Christ Jesus have been baptized into His death?

4 Therefore we have been buried with Him through baptism into death, in order that as Christ was raised from the dead through the glory of the Father, so we too might walk in newness of life.

5 For if we have become united with Him in the likeness of His death, certainly we shall be also in the likeness of His resurrection,

6 knowing this, that our old self was crucified with Him, that our body of sin might be done away with, that we should no longer be slaves to sin;

7 for he who has died is freed from sin.

8 Now if we have died with Christ, we believe that we shall also live with Him,

9 knowing that Christ, having been raised from the dead, is never to die again; death no longer is master over Him.

10 For the death that He died, He died to sin, once for all; but the life that He lives, He lives to God.

11 Even so consider yourselves to be dead to sin, but alive to God in Christ Jesus.

12 Therefore do not let sin reign in your mortal body that you should obey its lusts,

13 and do not go on presenting the members of your body to sin as instruments of unrighteousness; but present yourselves to God as those alive from the dead, and your members as instruments of righteousness to God.

14 For sin shall not be master over you, for you are not under law, but under grace.

15 What then? Shall we sin because we are not under law but under grace? May it never be!

16 Do you not know that when you present yourselves to someone as slaves for obedience, you are slaves of the one whom you obey, either of sin resulting in death, or of obedience resulting in righteousness?

17 But thanks be to God that though you were slaves of sin, you became obedient from the heart to that form of teaching to which you were committed,

18 and having been freed from sin, you became slaves of righteousness.

19 I am speaking in human terms because of the weakness of your flesh. For just as you presented your members as slaves to impurity and to lawless-

ness, resulting in further lawlessness, so now present your members as slaves to righteousness, resulting in sanctification.

20 For when you were slaves of sin, you were freed in regard to righteousness.

21 Therefore what benefit were you then deriving from the things of which you are now ashamed? For the outcome of those things is death.

22 But now having been freed from sin and enslaved to God, you derive your benefit, resulting in sanctification, and the outcome, eternal life.

23 For the wages of sin is death, but the free gift of God is eternal life in Christ Jesus our Lord.

Now go back and mark the following words in a distinctive way:

a. sin	e. reign
b. die (d), dead, death	f. life, live(s)
c. slave(s), enslaved	g. obey, obedience
d. free(d)	

That is all you need to do for today. If you have time, read Romans 6 through several more times—aloud!

– D A Y   F O U R –

Today I want you to continue to observe Romans 6 so that you see for yourself exactly what God is saying.

I could explain it all to you, but how would you know if what I was saying was right or wrong? You wouldn't, unless you knew for yourself what the text said. Although this is time-consuming labor, it will reap a wonderful harvest. "The hard-working farmer ought to be the first to receive his share of the crops. Consider what I say, for the Lord will give you understanding in everything" (2 Timothy 2:6-7).

With that word of exhortation, let me give you your assignment. Take the words: *sin; die(d), dead,* or *death;* and *slave(s)* or *enslaved* that you marked yesterday, and list everything you observed in the text about each one. For instance, you would list everything that you observed about sin, like this:

Sin:
1. We are not to continue in it.
2. We died to sin.
3. _____

Now it's your turn. Write in the following space, but if you run out of space, use a notebook.

Sin:

Die(d), dead, death:

Slave(s), enslaved:

How are you doing? Are you still overwhelmed by pain? Are you tempted to quit? Don't. The answers are coming. It just takes time.

— D A Y   F I V E —

When you grasp the truths of Romans 6, you will understand the great victory God wrought for you through Calvary. It will transform the way you walk.

As you read through Romans 6, you will find the word *baptism*. Theologians debate whether this refers to water baptism or to our identification with Christ. However, that debate doesn't serve the purpose of this book. Whether by water or by salvation, Paul simply wants us to see our identification with the Lord Jesus Christ.

1. Read through Romans 6 again, and mark each phrase *with Christ* or *with Him* in a distinctive color or with a symbol.

2. Now read Romans 6:1-11. What have we been baptized or united into? Take into consideration all of the *with Christ* and *with Him* phrases you just marked. Be as specific as the text.

3. Write out what your identification with Jesus Christ has personally wrought for you. Then take a moment and thank God for what He's done. You are loved.

– D A Y   S I X –

Living in unwavering obedience to truth, no matter how you feel, is the key to victory over any problem. Mental assent is not enough, you must do what God says you are to do.

There are no shortcuts to healing. There are fundamental truths we must know and embrace. Our identification with Christ in His death, burial, and resurrection is one of those fundamental truths that will bring healing. Our identification with Christ brings newness of life. In the week to come, we are going to begin to understand some of the glorious benefits of this new life that is ours.

Let's return to Romans 6. There is yet more you need to see. Ask the Father to take the veil off these truths and to engrave them in your heart so you might become a living epistle known and read by all men (2 Corinthians 3:2).

1. Take the remaining words you marked in Romans 6, and make a list of everything you learn from these key words: free(d); reign; life, live(s); obey, obedience. These truths belong to every child of God. Don't forget that!

Free(d):

Reign:

Life, live(s):

Obey, obedience:

2. What are God's commands or exhortations to the believer in Romans 6? List them.

3. In Romans 6:15-23 Paul contrasts two kinds of slaves. List these and note what you learn from the text regarding each.

4. Which category do you fit in? How do you know?

— D A Y   S E V E N —

When people have been deeply wounded, they often feel as if they have no worth, no value as human beings. Feelings or thoughts like this do not come from God. They have their origin in Satan—the father of lies, the accuser, the destroyer. As we will see later, Satan's primary target is the mind. It is for this reason that Ephesians 6 tells us the Christian's armor includes the helmet of salvation.

When we understand our salvation, we see our purpose as a human being. We were created in God's image, marred though we may be. Through salvation, the work of the Holy Spirit, and the transforming power of the Word of God, a gradual transformation will take place conforming us to the image of His Son.

In our last day of study for this week, I want you to focus on the truth of John 15:16.

1. Write out John 15:16.

2. From observing what the verse says and without reading anything into it, what do you learn about the child of God? List your insights below.

3. According to this verse, does your life as a child of God have worth and purpose? As you answer this question, forget how you feel, what you think about yourself, and what anyone else has said about you.

4. Write out a prayer to God. In your prayer make a commitment to live in accordance with the truth you have seen in His Word. Remember, those who hear God's Word and don't live accordingly delude themselves and miss God's blessing.

MEMORY VERSE

You did not choose Me, but I chose you, and appointed you, that you should go and bear fruit, and that your fruit should remain, that whatever you ask of the Father in My name, He may give to you.

JOHN 15:16

SMALL-GROUP DISCUSSION QUESTIONS

In week four our lesson gave us new insight into the cost of a provision for the healing of all of our hurts that are a result of sin.

We saw clearly the way in which Jesus provided for our wholeness through His life, His death, and now through His present ministry of intercession on our behalf.

And we learned that not only is He our High Priest but that He has been touched with the feelings of our infirmities—He understands because He has been there.

Again we talked of the fact that although all of the provision is there, it is our part to act in faith, take God at His Word, and appropriate it into our lives on a daily basis.

1. Not only is the Crucifixion a vital part of the gospel, there is another key ingredient to the gospel. Without this part of the gospel, we would still be dead in our trespasses and sins. What is the key part of the gospel?
2. What two vital truths does Christ's resurrection testify to?
3. Explain the significance of each of the truths in question 2.
4. What is the essence of the truths you have learned in Romans 6?
5. What is the key to victory over a problem? Is mental assent enough, or is there more to being victorious over a sin, a problem, than just agreeing with what God says?

6. What are some of the commands that God gives to the believer in Romans 6?

7. What did you learn from Paul's contrast of two slaves in Romans 6?

8. What has your identification with Jesus Christ made true for you?

9. Because we belong to Him, our lives have purpose. What marvelous truth did you learn from John 15:16?

10. In light of this lesson, are there any wrong concepts you have had simply because you did not fully understand all that being "in Christ" meant? How do you plan to deal with these to correct them? How do you plan to move forward in the truth?

GOD IS IN CONTROL, AND HE CARES

— DAY ONE —

A re you hurting because of your past? I understand. Mine tormented me until I learned the truths I'm about to teach you.

Last week you saw two key truths that are fundamental for dealing with the past. Let me review these. First, you are identified in Jesus' death and resurrection. This identification sets you free from slavery to sin so that you can be a slave of righteousness. Second, you were chosen by God. Mystery though it may be and hard to comprehend with finite minds, we didn't choose Him; He chose us. When He chose us, He had a plan. This truth is seen when He says: "You did not choose Me, but I chose you, and appointed you, that you should go and bear fruit, and that your fruit should remain, that whatever you ask of the Father in My name, He may give to you" (John 15:16).

The bottom line of these two truths is this: Once you've been set free from slavery to sin, you have a purpose in life. Your life has eternal value, not because of anything you are or did, but because God in His wondrous grace chose you to be His forever.

Are you asking, But what about my past? How can my life be of any value?

That, my friend, may be what you think, but I can tell you it is not what God thinks. Aren't you glad?

You have one, and only one, assignment for today. Pray that God will rip the veil off your eyes and show you how He can redeem the seemingly destructive traumas of the past and use them for your good and His glory. Write out your prayer in the provided space.

– D A Y   T W O –

Romans 8:28 is familiar to many Christians, and yet I wonder if we quote it glibly, without comprehending the depth of its meaning and the context in which it is given.

God is using this verse to sustain me in one of the greatest traumas of my life. I'm not at liberty to share my hurt, but let me assure you it has nothing to do with my precious husband or with our relationship. I simply want you to know that I live by what I am about to share with you.

Printed out for you is Romans 8:28-39. Read it carefully.

1. Mark the following key words in a distinctive way: *God, Christ,* or *Christ Jesus.* Also mark all pronouns referring to the Godhead.

2. Mark every personal pronoun referring to the child of God (*us, we, whom, those, these*).

3. When you finish marking your key words, list everything you learn about God and about Jesus Christ at the end of the text. (You will use the right hand margin tomorrow.) Please don't do anything more today.

▶ ROMANS 8:28-39

28 And we know that God causes all things to work together for good to those who love God, to those who are called according to His purpose.

29 For whom He foreknew, He also predestined to become conformed to the image of His Son, that He might be the first-born among many brethren;

30 and whom He predestined, these He also called; and whom He called, these He also justified; and whom He justified, these He also glorified.

31 What then shall we say to these things? If God is for us, who is against us?

32 He who did not spare His own Son, but

delivered Him up for us all, how will He not also with Him freely give us all things?

33 Who will bring a charge against God's elect? God is the one who justifies;

34 who is the one who condemns? Christ Jesus is He who died, yes, rather who was raised, who is at the right hand of God, who also intercedes for us.

35 Who shall separate us from the love of Christ? Shall tribulation, or distress, or persecution, or famine, or nakedness, or peril, or sword?

36 Just as it is written, "FOR THY SAKE WE ARE BEING PUT TO DEATH ALL DAY LONG; WE WERE CONSIDERED AS SHEEP TO BE SLAUGHTERED."

37 But in all these things we overwhelmingly conquer through Him who loved us.

38 For I am convinced that neither death, nor life, nor angels, nor principalities, nor things present, nor things to come, nor powers,

39 nor height, nor depth, nor any other

created thing, shall be able to separate us from

the love of God, which is in Christ Jesus our

Lord.

— D A Y   T H R E E —

So often we quote or read Romans 8:28, "And we know that God causes all things to work together for good, to those who love God, to those who are called according to His purpose." Then we stop there. Although a period comes after verse 28, the thought still continues. Our question should be, What is the good that God promises to bring about in our lives?

You can answer that question by observing the text of Romans 8:28-39.

1. Read through the passage from Romans 8 that you marked yesterday.

2. In the right-hand margin, list everything you observed as a result of marking the personal pronouns which refer to the child of God. These are truths which belong to you, if you belong to Him. And if you don't yet, you can know that God wants you in His family.

3. If you are hurting terribly, or if there is a great deal of bitterness and unforgiveness in your heart, then, Beloved, this assignment may be hard to do at this point. I understand. Do the best you can—give it a good try. In several weeks we will deal with bitterness and unforgiveness. Now study Romans 8:28-39 and write out the good that God intends to accomplish in your life through everything that has happened to you. Use the following space.

4. What questions come to your mind when you read Romans 8:28-39? List them in the space that follows. (For example: How could God cause incest to work together for my good?)

– D A Y   F O U R –

What is the good God promises to bring about in your life? Christlikeness. God wants every believer to be like His Son. Romans 8:29 tells us that God foreknew us. In knowing us beforehand He predestined, or marked out before, that we should be conformed to the image of His son. Conformation to the image of Jesus Christ is achieved through three things: our proper relationship to God, our response to the Word of God, and the suffering which attends the life of every child of God. These will be our topics of study for the remainder of the week.

First, let's take a look at how God uses His Word to conform us to the image of Jesus Christ. Take a minute to read 2 Corinthians 3 in your Bible. In this chapter Paul is contrasting the old covenant, which was the law put on tablets of stone, with the new covenant of grace, which is written upon our hearts by the indwelling Holy Spirit.

In 2 Corinthians 3 Paul explains that when a person comes to Jesus Christ, a veil is taken away. This veil is the old covenant, a covenant which the Jews misunderstood. They thought they could be saved by keeping the law. Although salvation had always been by grace, the Jews misunderstood the purpose of the law and felt that by keeping it they could make themselves acceptable to God. "For not knowing about God's righteousness, and seeking to establish their own, they did not subject themselves to the righteousness of God" (Romans 10:3). They sought a righteousness by works. They didn't understand their inability to be righteous.

Because they lacked poverty of spirit, they could not see that God saves us: "Not on the basis of deeds which we have done in righteousness, but according to His mercy, by the washing of regeneration and renewing by the Holy Spirit, whom He poured out upon us richly through Jesus Christ our Savior, that being justified by His grace we might be made heirs according to the hope of eternal life" (Titus 3:5-7).

O Beloved, if you think you have in any way earned or deserved salvation, you are blind to truth. When a person understands and accepts that salvation is by pure grace—unearned, unmerited favor—given to man because of what Jesus Christ accomplished at Calvary, then the veil is taken away. Faith alone brings a person into the kingdom of God.

But that's just the beginning. God not only saves you, He also begins to transform you into the image He intended for man when He created

Adam and Eve. An image unmarred by sin. How is that image restored in you and me, who once lived in sin? It begins at salvation with the indwelling of the Holy Spirit, and it continues as we study and obey the Word of God.

Look up the following verses, and write out what you learn about how we are cleansed and transformed. By the way, the English transliteration of the Greek word for *transformation* is *metamorphoō*. Interesting, isn't it, when you stop and think about the metamorphosis that takes place when a caterpillar is changed into a butterfly.

1. 2 Corinthians 3:18

2. Romans 12:2

3. Ephesians 5:25-27 (Watch carefully what Christ does for the church. Note the *how* and *why* of it all.)

Well, dear student, that is enough for today. Tomorrow we will take a look at how suffering is used of God to transform us into the image of His Son.

— D A Y   F I V E —

Suffering is one of God's primary means of conforming us to the image of His Son, Jesus Christ. As the God-man, Jesus suffered. As children of God, we will suffer.

When I suffer, it's always a comfort to know I'm not alone and my suffering has a purpose. Let me give you some verses that should greatly encourage you, as they have me.

The author of Hebrews writes of Jesus: "Although He was a Son, He learned obedience from the things which He suffered" (Hebrews 5:8).

Philippians 1:29 states: "For to you it has been granted for Christ's sake, not only to believe in Him, but also to suffer for His sake."

Romans 8:16-18 assures us that: "The Spirit Himself bears witness with our spirit that we are children of God, and if children, heirs also, heirs of God and fellow heirs with Christ, if indeed we suffer with Him in order that we may also be glorified with Him. For I consider that the sufferings of this present time are not worthy to be compared with the glory that is to be revealed to us."

Suffering and glory go together. You can't have one without the other. Thus, God likens our suffering to the purifying of silver and gold. Neither metal is pure in its natural state. Both are mixed with all sorts of things which make them impure.

Isn't that the way it is with us? We are born with a sin nature that constantly attracts all sorts of impurities: thoughts, beliefs, destructive actions, and habits. We are influenced by our environment—an environment permeated with sin.

Silver and gold need to be refined before they reveal their beauty. So do we! The process of refining includes the melting down of the metal by fires designed not to destroy the metal, but to bring forth its beauty.

Let's look at how silver is purified. The silver is crushed into small pieces and placed into a crucible. The silversmith places the crucible over the fire that has been prepared to just the right degree of heat, and then he watches carefully as the silver melts.

Eventually impurities will rise to the top of the crucible. These are scraped off carefully by the silversmith. Then an even hotter fire is built. Once again the silver is subjected to the heat. Now, under this new intensity of fire, more and different impurities are released.

The silversmith never leaves the silver unattended in the fire, lest the silver be damaged by too much heat. Each time the fire is increased and the impurities are removed, the silversmith bends over the crucible to look at himself in melted silver. At first his image is dim...his face barely discernible. However, with each new fire his image becomes more distinct. When he finally sees himself clearly, he knows all the impurities are gone. The refining is complete.

So it is with you, Beloved. God breaks you and puts you into the crucible of suffering for one purpose and one purpose alone—to make you into His image. He is preparing you for glory. Whether you have known it or not, God has been there through every trial, pain, and hurt. He has carefully watched so that it would not destroy you, all the while knowing that eventually it would work together for your good.

Listen to His words: "In this you greatly rejoice, even though now for a little while, if necessary, you have been distressed by various trials, that the proof of your faith, being more precious than gold which is perishable, even though tested by fire, may be found to result in praise and glory and honor at the revelation of Jesus Christ" (1 Peter 1:6-8).

Learn to see every trial—past, present, and future—as part of God's refining process to make you like Jesus.

The question that confronts you is, How will you respond to suffering? Not only the suffering which awaits you, but also the suffering which you have endured in the past? Will you let it embitter you or transform you? Will you hold on to the dross, or will you be made like Jesus?

Every trial of life is a test of your faith because with each trial you are called upon to make a decision. The decision is, Will you believe God and, thus, respond in the way He says to respond, or will you cling to the dross of independent disobedience and, therefore, sin in the unbelief of the flesh?

Let me take you to 2 Corinthians 4:7-12. (Note: The phrase "but we have this treasure" refers to the indwelling of the Spirit through the New Covenant.) Listen to the Word of God:

▶ 2 CORINTHIANS 4:7-12

7 But we have this treasure in earthen vessels, that the surpassing greatness of the power may be of God and not from ourselves;

8 we are afflicted in every way, but not crushed; perplexed, but not despairing;

9 persecuted, but not forsaken; struck down, but not destroyed;

10 always carrying about in the body the dying of Jesus, that the life of Jesus also may be manifested in our body.

11 For we who live are constantly being delivered over to death for Jesus' sake, that the life of Jesus also may be manifested in our mortal flesh.

12 So death works in us, but life in you.

1. Mark the following words in the passage you just read from 2 Corinthians: *life, death, dying.*

2. According to 2 Corinthians 4:7-12 why are we delivered over to death, to difficult situations of life?

3. What did you notice about each calamitous situation mentioned here? Write out your insights.

Do you begin to see how God can use all that you have endured to give hope and life to others? If you will believe God, trust Him, and cling to Him in faith, can you see how your obedience can be used to minister life to others?

And how are you going to walk in such a way so as to live this out? Paul goes on to tell you in 2 Corinthians 4:16-18.

4. Look up 2 Corinthians 4:16-18, and write it out.

5. Write out what you must do if you are going to walk in faith's victory.

Your healing is dependent upon your response. I say all of this neither to discourage you...nor to cause you to throw this book across the room in anger. At this point, you may not think you can handle what I am saying.

Be patient. Don't walk away. We have progressed this far. Finish the course you have begun. Don't let the one who would destroy you hold you captive. Remember the devil is a liar and a murderer (John 8:44) who would keep you from your Great Physician and His healing balm.

— D A Y   S I X —

Suffering will either refine us or it will embitter us. We decide. Sometimes when we suffer, we think God doesn't care about us. Otherwise, why would He allow it? Why doesn't He do something about our pain?

I will never forget a woman with whom I shared the gospel. Oh, how she was hurting...and I hurt with her when I heard her story.

I met her when I was out doing door-to-door evangelism with some people from our church. As we sat in her living room talking, I could not help but notice the lines on her face that belied her age. Her life seemed in as much disarray as her home. Hopelessness hung in the air. As I shared the gospel, telling her of her need of the Savior and the love of God, bitterness spilled from her lips, "When God gives me back my baby, then I'll listen to Him."

My verbal witness came to a halt as I probed to try to find out what she meant. Her baby had died in a fire. I listened and then I shared that God understood. He, too, had lost His Son. But I couldn't convince her that because God gave up His Son, she could someday be reunited with hers. Anger had hardened her heart, and she missed the healing that God alone could bring. A bitter woman saw me to the door.

Nothing can separate us from the love of God, according to Romans 8:35-39. The tribulations, distresses, and persecutions that come into our lives are not meant to destroy us. They are designed to drive us into His everlasting arms of love. In His sovereignty, God has allowed suffering. The One who sits upon the throne of thrones reigns supremely. He does "according to his will in the army of heaven, and among the inhabitants of the earth" (Daniel 4:35, KJV). He holds you in His omnipotent hands.

God is love, and He loves you with an everlasting love. Therefore, everything that comes into your life must be filtered through His fingers of love. No one can touch you, speak to you, look at you, or do anything to you without His permission. If adversity comes into your life, it comes with His permission (Isaiah 45:7). And if it comes, it will work together for your good. It will be used to conform you into His image. It will not keep you from the kingdom of heaven.

> Whom He predestined, these He also called; and whom He called, these He also justified; and whom He justified, these He also glorified.... Who shall separate us from the love of Christ? Shall tribulation, or distress, or persecution, or famine, or nakedness, or peril, or sword? Just as it is written, "FOR THY SAKE WE ARE BEING PUT TO DEATH ALL DAY LONG; WE WERE CONSIDERED AS SHEEP TO BE SLAUGHTERED." But in all these things we overwhelmingly conquer through Him who loved us. For I am convinced that neither death, nor life, nor angels, nor principalities, nor things present, nor things to come, nor powers, nor height, nor depth, nor any other created thing, shall be able to separate us from the love of God, which is in Christ Jesus our Lord. (Romans 8:30,35-39)

Whatever God allows to come into your life, Beloved, you can know it is not designed to embitter, disfigure, or destroy you. It is permitted by a loving God for the purpose of conforming you into the image of His Son, Jesus Christ.

For further proof, look up the following verses and write them out. Then think about them.

1. Write out the last three words of 1 John 4:8. This is an unchanging attribute of God. Therefore, He will never act apart from what you learn about Him from this verse.

2. Daniel 4:34-35

3. Isaiah 45:5-7 (The word *evil* [KJV] or *calamity* [NASB] means *adversity.*)

4. Psalm 103:19

5. Deuteronomy 32:39

6. Jeremiah 19:11 (What God says of Israel, His chosen people, I believe He says of you, His chosen.)

My friend, embrace these truths in faith.

— D A Y S E V E N —

God, in His sovereignty, chose us and ordained that we should go and bear fruit. He promises that all things in our lives will work together for good and will be used to conform us to the image of His Son.

In our final and brief day of study for this week, I want us to look at *when* we were chosen by God and at *what*, if anything, caused God to choose us.

1. Read Romans 8:29. According to this verse, for what did God predestine us?

2. Now read Ephesians 1:3-6.

▶ EPHESIANS 1:3-6

3 Blessed be the God and Father of our Lord Jesus Christ, who has blessed us with every spiritual blessing in the heavenly places in Christ,

4 just as He chose us in Him before the foundation of the world, that we should be holy and blameless before Him. In love

5 He predestined us to adoption as sons through Jesus Christ to Himself, according to the kind intention of His will,

6 to the praise of the glory of His grace, which He freely bestowed on us in the Beloved.

3. Whenever you read the Word, always ask yourself the "5 Ws and an H": *who, what, when, where, why,* and *how.* To help you get into practice, ask and answer the "5 Ws and an H" concerning these verses. Examine them from every possible angle. Ask: Who was speaking? To whom? Who blessed? Who chose? Cover each "W" and every "H" you can in these verses. Write out your insights on the next page.

If you need more space, use an extra piece of paper.

4. In a single sentence, summarize what you learned regarding when God chose you and what His purpose was.

5. How does what you have seen today relate to your past and to what you learned from Romans 8:28-39? If you do not see any relationship, then be honest...but do not give up.

There is much more for us to see on this subject of dealing with our past. I believe the Lord will greatly use the truths that we will see in the coming week to minister healing to you in a very special way. Or if you don't need healing, I know God will use these truths to help you minister to others.

My prayer for you, beloved and diligent student, is that God will show you how precious you are in His sight, not because of who or what you are, but simply because of who He is and because of the unmerited favor He has chosen to bestow upon you as a vessel of His mercy.

While I say all of this, I must give you the other side of the coin. There are those who accept what God is doing and respond in obedience to the Word, but there are others who do not. They refuse to let go of the impurities of bitterness, hate, anger, revenge, and other things which hurts can bring. Instead of relinquishing these in faith, they cling to them, even in the fire of increased suffering. The result is that they become what God calls rejected or reprobate silver.

This is what happened in Jeremiah's day when the people refused God's balm, God's healing. Listen to God's word to Jeremiah regarding these people: "'I have made you an assayer and a tester among My people, that you may know and assay their way.' All of them are stubbornly rebellious…they, all of them, are corrupt. The bellows blow fiercely, the lead is consumed by the fire; in vain the refining goes on, but the wicked are not separated. They call them rejected silver, because the LORD has rejected them" (6:27-30).

If you and I do not respond to the truths of God's Word and allow it to transform us into His image, then God can do nothing more with us. Don't let this happen to you. If you do, you will never know His healing.

You can come through all of this, conformed into the image of Jesus Christ—because of His life, death, and resurrection. You can because Jesus lives to intercede for you. Remember He understands you. "Although He was a Son, He learned obedience from the things which He suffered. And having been made perfect, He became to all those who obey Him the source of eternal salvation" (Hebrews 5:8-9).

MEMORY VERSE

And we know that God causes all things to work together for good to those who love God, to those who are called according to His purpose.

ROMANS 8:28

SMALL-GROUP DISCUSSION QUESTIONS

In week five we saw the significance of the Resurrection. The study gave us great insight into what is actually ours because He was raised from the dead so that we do not have to live in our trespasses and sins and because we are identified with Him in His death, burial, and resurrection by faith in the finished work of Christ.

We learned we are not only saved from the penalty of sin but also from the power of sin. Sin no longer reigns!

We also looked at the awesome fact that we were chosen by God—chosen to be His beloved children!

1. What two key truths did we learn last week that are the basis for you to be able to deal with your past?

2. This week in your study what did you see that God is in control of?

3. Since He is in control of all things, how does this apply to you? Did you come to God on your own, or did God have something to do with it?

4. When were you chosen by God? How?

5. What are the truths that you saw in Romans 8:28-39 that belong to the child of God?

6. If you were chosen before the foundation of the world and if what you learned in Romans 8 is true, then what is true about all of the things that make up your past?

   a. Is any of these a surprise to God?

   b. Can He use these situations? How do you know?

7. What is the good that God promises to bring about by using all that has happened in your life?

8. From what you learned in the Scriptures when you studied cleansing and transformation, how are you to be transformed and cleansed?

9. What is one of the primary means used by God to conform us into the image of His Son?

10. What do the truths that you have learned this week mean to you on a daily basis? How can you apply these truths to your life moment by moment?

GOD IS THERE!

I used to ache because I had not come to know Jesus Christ earlier. I thought of what might have been if I had heard the gospel before I ever divorced Tom. I thought of what could have been for my children had I not gone into immorality. I lived with the ghosts of "if only," and I was miserable. And then, through the transforming power of the Word of God, I was set free.

As I immersed myself in the Bible, I saw that God saved me when it pleased Him. I saw that I was chosen in Christ Jesus before the foundation of the world to be adopted as His child. But I also saw that the timing of my salvation was God's doing. In God's sovereignty, I would not be saved until I was twenty-nine—already divorced and caught in the snare of immorality. God knew all of that! And in His sovereignty He planned that *even the timing of my salvation* would work together for good.

How awesome!

Many hurt, as I did, because they have lived in open rebellion to the clear commandments of God. They have shaken their fists in God's face. Instead of allowing God's law to keep them from sin until they came to faith in Jesus Christ, they insisted on doing their own thing. And they reaped an awful harvest! A harvest which they are ashamed of once they come to know the Lord Jesus Christ, as Romans 6 says.

They weep and live with "if onlys." Although Jesus Christ paid for their sin at Calvary, putting it behind His back and remembering it no more, they keep it ever before their eyes.

They wear the memory of their sin like a black shroud of mourning, keeping others from seeing the radiance that His forgiveness should bring. Grief over past sins saps their strength. They are weak and even impotent in serving God. They need either to hear or to be reminded of God's Word given to His people when they were mourning their sins: "Do not be grieved, for the joy of the LORD is your strength" (Nehemiah 8:10).

Is there hope for those who are saved yet who are still haunted by the ghosts of past sins? For those who feel as if they are second-class citizens in the kingdom of God? For those who have a hard time seeing how God can use them because of their past sins?

Yes!

1. Read, once again, Ephesians 1:3-6. You might want to review the "5 Ws and an H" which you observed when you studied these verses last week.

2. In Galatians 1:11-17 Paul refers briefly to his conversion. Read this passage carefully, and write out what you learn about the timing of Paul's salvation.

— D A Y   T W O —

I have a note written to me on lined paper. The side with the holes is ragged and fringed where it was hastily torn from a three-ring notebook on January 17, 1986.

Your teaching tonight has so freed me to believe that God has chosen me from before there was time to be His—knowing full well that my life would be so full of sin.

Before I was saved, I was an adulteress, stole the man who lived next door to my parents from his wife and children, had his child out of wedlock and finally succeeded in getting him to marry me when our child was two years old. When I came to the Lord, I was devastated to realize what pain and suffering my sin caused so many, but especially how I had grieved my Lord. God has redeemed much of the hurt to so many and in His miraculous ways has brought us to a place of loving one another, but I still have felt that He let me slip in the back door and that never could I be truly special to Him.

But, oh Kay, I know that He chose me with full knowledge of how wretched I would be and that I am now called holy and blameless by the blood of my precious Jesus.

Here is the testimony of a woman who has come to know the truth, and, in the knowing, to be set free. Free because she believed God!

O Beloved, are you believing God?

Take what you learned yesterday about God's timing of salvation and write out how you would help people deal with the trauma of their past. Be as specific as you can in your answer.

— D A Y   T H R E E —

What about those who are hurting because of things they couldn't control?

Those who have been mentally, emotionally, physically abused by others…parents or people they trusted?

Those who are hurting from bitterness and anger because they don't like who they are—their bodies, their personalities? Or those who have suffered rejection because of physical handicaps or tendencies to be too fat or too skinny, rejections that might have come in a dozen different but painfully real forms?

Those who are bulimic or anorexic and yet refuse to deal with the reality that they are destroying their bodies?

Those victimized, molested, sodomized by perverted, twisted, ungodly sinners?

Is healing possible for all these?

Yes, yes, yes!

There is a balm in Gilead, a Great Physician there.

If you are going to say, "No, these are psychological needs which *only* psychology can help," then you must also say that God could not deal with these types of hurts before the advent of psychology around one hundred years ago. You would have to say that the Word of God was impotent under the ministry of the Holy Spirit. And, if you held to this premise, you would elevate man to omniscience and omnipotence. You would delay emotional healing until man finally evolved to a place where he, in his own wisdom, could gain insight into the intricacies of the soul of man. And then I would have to ask if there is a permanent cure apart from God?

Can we debate whether or not the Bible has the answers for any and every situation of life—even the traumas which have come from the hands of ungodly sinners? I honestly don't believe we can and still maintain a faith pleasing to God. For "without faith it is impossible to please Him, for he who comes to God must believe that He is, and that He is a rewarder of those who seek Him" (Hebrews 11:6). God's Word is sufficient, it holds the cure.

God is Jehovah-rapha, the God who heals.

Where does one begin the healing process? With an understanding of the character and sovereignty of God. However, it does not end there. Many aren't healed when they could be because they don't understand God's watchcare in bringing us to salvation. Nor do they understand the thoroughness and completeness of our salvation. Spiritually they resemble street people, picking up the world's trash in order to sustain life.

Tomorrow we will begin soaking up the truths of Psalm 139. Today, keep crying out in faith, "Heal me, O Lord, and I will be healed," and know that whatever you ask in His name He will do. What better prayer could you pray in the name of your Jehovah-rapha than this!

Speaking of our need to pray for healing, I think it would be profitable for you to look up Luke 11:1-13, read it carefully, and answer the following questions:

1. What is the main theme of this passage? Or to put it another way, what is the main thing Jesus is dealing with in these verses?

2. What is the point Jesus is making regarding this theme in verses 5-10? (Hint: *Ask, seek,* and *knock* are all in the present tense in the Greek, which denotes continuous or habitual action.)

3. What point is Jesus making in verses 11-13?

4. What can you learn from these verses about praying for healing?

— D A Y   F O U R —

One of the key passages for healing the traumas I mentioned yesterday is Psalm 139. This psalm is printed out for you.

Your assignment for today is twofold. Don't fail to do exactly what you are instructed to do. This will be the turning point for many of you.

1. Read Psalm 139 aloud. Concentrate on what you are reading, on what the psalmist is saying. Read this psalm at least three times. Remember to read aloud each time because when you read something aloud repeatedly, you'll automatically memorize it. Speaking and hearing it causes your mind to retain it.

2. Read through the psalm a fourth time. This time mark each *Thou* and *Thee*. Then at the end of today's assignment, list everything you learn from the use of *Thou* and *Thee*.

▶ PSALM 139

¹ O LORD, Thou hast searched me and known me.

² Thou dost know when I sit down and when I rise up; Thou dost understand my thought from afar.

3 Thou dost scrutinize my path and my lying down, and art intimately acquainted with all my ways.

4 Even before there is a word on my tongue, behold, O LORD, Thou dost know it all.

5 Thou hast enclosed me behind and before, and laid Thy hand upon me.

6 Such knowledge is too wonderful for me; it is too high, I cannot attain to it.

7 Where can I go from Thy Spirit? Or where can I flee from Thy presence?

8 If I ascend to heaven, Thou art there; if I make my bed in Sheol, behold, Thou art there.

9 If I take the wings of the dawn, if I dwell in the remotest part of the sea,

10 Even there Thy hand will lead me, and Thy right hand will lay hold of me.

11 If I say, "Surely the darkness will overwhelm me, and the light around me will be night,"

12 Even the darkness is not dark to Thee, and the night is as bright as the day. Darkness and light are alike to Thee.

13 For Thou didst form my inward parts; Thou didst weave me in my mother's womb.

14 I will give thanks to Thee, for I am fearfully and wonderfully made; wonderful are Thy works, and my soul knows it very well.

15 My frame was not hidden from Thee, when I was made in secret, and skillfully wrought in the depths of the earth.

16 Thine eyes have seen my unformed substance; and in Thy book they were all written, the days that were ordained for me, when as yet there was not one of them.

17 How precious also are Thy thoughts to me, O God! How vast is the sum of them!

18 If I should count them, they would outnumber the sand. When I awake, I am still with Thee.

19 O that Thou wouldst slay the wicked, O God; depart from me, therefore, men of bloodshed.

20 For they speak against Thee wickedly, and Thine enemies take Thy name in vain.

21 Do I not hate those who hate Thee, O LORD? And do I not loathe those who rise up against Thee?

22 I hate them with the utmost hatred; they have become my enemies.

23 Search me, O God, and know my heart; try me and know my anxious thoughts;

24 And see if there be any hurtful way in me, and lead me in the everlasting way.

– D A Y F I V E –

Once again we are going to spend the day in Psalm 139. This psalm will be our focus for the remainder of this week.

If you will carefully and diligently do all God has laid upon my heart for you, I believe your relationship with the Father will take on a new depth of intimacy and understanding. Therefore, I am not going to be writing or sharing much with you because the psalm will speak for itself.

1. Read through Psalm 139 again.
   a. Mark each use of the words *Thy* and *Thine*.
   b. List in the following space the words that *Thy* and *Thine* modify (e.g., Spirit, hand, etc.).
   c. Next to each phrase you recorded, write what you learn and how it personally relates to you. For example: Thy hand has been laid on me—This means God knows me personally, has touched my life. He has not left me alone.

2. As you read through Psalm 139 again, remember it was written for you. Read it aloud three times. Don't let your mind wander as you read. Ask God to speak to you, to let you see what He is saying about you. Thank Him today for what you are seeing.

– D A Y   S I X –

In Psalm 139 God reveals different aspects of His character or attributes. I want you to see these on your own before I share them with you. Therefore, before you read any further—

1. List what you learn about God from this psalm. Write out your insights as if you were describing what you have learned about God to someone else.

2. At the end of this book you will find a list of the attributes of God. Read through them carefully. As you come across an attribute that is revealed in this psalm, record it, along with the verse in which you saw this attribute.

3. From the list of God's attributes at the end of this book, what did you learn about the character of God that could help you deal with your hurts? Write it out.

4. Psalm 139 reveals much about God, but it also has much to say about us. Draw a little stick figure over every reference to *I, me, mine, my.* List below all you learn from marking these personal pronouns. Put a star beside those that you can personalize. Put a question mark by those truths that you are not sure you want to believe.

5. If you are disappointed in your parents, if you are hurting because of what your father or mother has done to you or because of what they have failed to be to you, I want to ask you two questions:
   a. Who allowed you to have the parents that you have?

   b. If your parents have failed you, if they have not been the kind of parents God wanted them to be, what must you assume from our study of God's Word?

Think on these things, and we will deal with them in the weeks to come. Tomorrow we will look at a summary of Psalm 139.

– D A Y   S E V E N –

In the midst of the book of Psalms, Psalm 139 resounds like the triumphant clash of cymbals. Behold your God. Be awed with His all-encompassing love and care for you.

Before you were even formed in your mother's womb, you were His.

Taking the theme of God's sovereign love and care, Psalm 139 might be outlined as follows:

The Sovereign Love and Care of God as:
Verses 1-6	The Omniscient One
Verses 7-12	The Omnipresent One
Verses 13-18	The Creator-Sustainer
Verses 19-24	The Righteous Judge

How comforting to know that, because God is omniscient (all-knowing), He is intimately acquainted with all of your ways! Did you notice how the psalmist kept saying "Thou"? Our God who knows it all, who understands everything, has enclosed you behind and before. God is not far away, unconcerned, unaware of the events of your life, nor of your secret thoughts. He cares for you in such a way that He, *God Himself,* has laid His hand upon you. It is astonishing, isn't it, that you would be the object of concern to Almighty Elohim! He has inscribed you on the palms of His hands (Isaiah 49:16). He cannot forget you! Calvary's nail prints are there forever.

Remember that your Father God knows about everything that has ever been done to you! Remember also that He is the righteous Judge who will deal with those who have wounded you, His child.

But there's more. Not only does God know all that has happened to you, He was also there. You were never alone. Whether you recognized His presence or not, He was there. None can flee from His presence. He was there, my friend, when you felt as the psalmist, "Surely the darkness will overwhelm me, and the light around me will be night." He was there... protecting, keeping, preserving.

Your Creator did not bring you into existence only to abandon you. He is your Creator-Sustainer. Maybe you have spent your life wishing you had different parents, wondering what it would have been like had you had a mother and dad like a friend's.

Beloved, such wasted thinking will only make you more miserable. As you saw, God gave you your parents (Psalm 139:13-16). Your parents may have been far from God's example as a parent, but let go of those expectations. If you are angry, hurt, or disappointed, remember Romans 8:28 and 1 Corinthians 10:13. You may feel your parents are more than you can bear, but God has provided His way of escape. Cling to Him as the waistband clings to the waist of a man, and He will make you a person for praise, renown, and glory (Jeremiah 13:11).

Your life is not over. God ordained the number of days you are to live when as yet there was not one of them (Psalm 139:16). And in His sovereignty He has led you to this study to learn these truths. You are to believe. He has confronted you with His truth. Now you determine your healing. The balm is there. Will you apply it?

I want to share one more truth about your Creator-Sustainer. You may not like the way you look physically, but God has a purpose even in that. He says that you are "fearfully and wonderfully made." You may despise yourself simply because you are not built in the proportion you think you ought to be, or you may not like the shape of your face or the color of your eyes, but all of that has a purpose. Your frame was not hidden from God when you were skillfully wrought. His thoughts toward you are precious. God does not lie.

Finally we see God as the Righteous Judge. He is able to judge righteously because He is omniscient and omnipresent. Nothing has been hidden from Him. He will deal with the wicked.

God does not expect you to side with wickedness. Nor does He want you to keep company with those who hate Him. His enemies are to be yours. And yet you are to treat His enemies and yours the way He says to treat them. You will find your instructions in the New Testament in places like Matthew 5:44-48 and Romans 12:14-21.

Because God will righteously judge those who have hurt you, you do not have to deal out retribution to your enemies. Your enemies are His. Let Him deal with them. Your task is to forgive; His is to judge. We'll discuss the how and why of forgiveness later.

The psalm closes with your responsibility: Let God keep your heart pure by searching it and letting you know your anxious thoughts. He will show you any hurtful ways in your life so that you might deal with them and walk in His everlasting way. Isn't it wonderful to know that your Father will keep you pure for the asking?

Let me close with this word of exhortation. In the light of all the infallible truth of Psalm 139, won't you bow your knee in humble submission to the will of God and His sovereign ways, and "in everything give thanks; for this is God's will for you in Christ Jesus" (1 Thessalonians 5:18)? If you will, and if you will continue to walk in faithful obedience, you will find God's divine healing.

MEMORY VERSE

In everything give thanks; for this is God's will for you in
Christ Jesus.

1 THESSALONIANS 5:18

SMALL-GROUP DISCUSSION QUESTIONS

In week six we learned that God is sovereign, that He rules over all. In His
sovereignty He chose us before the foundation of the world.

His desire is to conform us into the image of Jesus Christ. This conformation and transformation will take place as we allow the Word of
God to work in us.

Since God is sovereign and since He says that all things work together
for good for those who love God, who are called according to His purpose, our past hurts, disappointments, tragedies, and failures are no surprise to Him. According to His Word, He will even use all of this to
conform us into the image of His Son.

1. If it is true that God is sovereign and in control and if He chose you
   before the foundation of the world to be His,

   a. was He surprised at the timing of your salvation?

   b. what did you learn about the timing of Paul's salvation?

2. In light of all that we have learned, was God taken off guard by anything that happened to you as a child? as a teen? as a young adult? as
   an adult? an elderly person? Is He able to use the different situations
   that occurred in each stage of your life, or have these events ruined
   your life? How do you know? How will He use each incident?

3. As you read and reread Psalm 139, what different aspects of God's
   character did you see, or which of His attributes were listed in the
   psalm?

4. From the truths of Psalm 139, who is it that God knows? How well?

5. What does He know about you? Does He know when you are hurting?

6. In Psalm 139 you see that God is always where? When you were hurt, where was God? Were you alone at that time?

7. We saw too that not only did He know all and not only was He everywhere, but He created us and He sustains us. In verse 14 what do you see that your response should be to the way He made you?

   a. Were there any accidents as He formed you in your mother's womb?

   b. If your parents felt you were a mistake or wished you were never born, what do you know from God's Word that would help you deal with this hurt? What must you choose to believe?

   c. Did God know who your parents were? Did He make a mistake in choosing your parents for you? Why do you think God allowed you to have the parents you have?

8. What did you learn about your God, the Righteous Judge?

9. At the close of Psalm 139, what do you learn about your responsibility?

10. What did you learn from Luke 11 about your healing?

11. What kind of gift did you see in Luke 11 that your Father would give you? If the answer to your persistent prayer is not what you think it should be, what did you learn in Luke 11 that you can rest in?

12. In light of this week's study, what is your response now to your home, your parents, your losses, your body, your hurts, your disappointments, and the tragedies of your past? of the future?

LETTING YOUR MIND BE RENEWED

− D A Y   O N E −

Have you ever stopped to think of how God could use the sins you have committed, the hurts you have suffered, the wounds you have endured, the rejection you have experienced, to minister to others?

There was a time in my beginning with Jesus when I became depressed over my past. The enemy continually brought before me "what-might-have-been." My mind became Satan's hunting ground as I thought about how things could have been different. Like so many others, I had my dreams and expectations of what life should be. In my dreams there was peace, love, security—a picture of a wonderfully romantic marriage, a happy *Father Knows Best* or *Cosby* type of family life. Trials? Yes. But tragedies? NO!

As these thoughts of what-might-have-been or what-could-have-been-if-only plagued me, I found my emotions careening seemingly out of control, doomed to crash, leaving me shattered. It was difficult to cope. I was consumed with regrets from the past…the future held nothing.

Can you relate, my friend? It's a little bit of hell, isn't it? You want what others have, and you feel life, or even God, has maliciously cheated you of happiness.

Do you look at those who failed you and know that your relationship is not what it should be or could be? Are you torn with a dichotomy of feelings? In one moment you want their love and approval. But in the next moment you want to turn on them because something triggers the memory of the past and of their failure to be what you expected them to be. Their failure eats at you like a painful ulcer.

How do you deal with such thoughts? Is there any spiritual balm that can heal the regrets of your past? Yes. Healing begins with understanding that God is in control.

All of your past has purpose in God's sovereign plan. However, Satan would have you believe otherwise. He is a liar, a murderer, the destroyer who, since the Garden of Eden, has continued to whisper in man's thoughts the suggestion that God does not care, that God does not want our good. And so, it is in your mind—in your thoughts—that the battle for your healing rages. And on this battleground the victory is won!

Think about what you have just read. Can you relate in any way? How? Write it out.

− D A Y   T W O −

As you know, my life is not free from hurts. But because I know the Word of God, I'm able to allow God to heal these hurts as they come. If my life were as I dreamed it would be, there would be no hurts, no suffering. However, my hurts enable me to relate to you, to understand where you are coming from. I can communicate to you in a way that lets you know you can live life as more than a conqueror. I can say with certainty that there is a healing balm in Gilead.

Do you realize that God refers to believers as a kingdom of priests? Look up the following verses and write them out.

1. Revelation 1:5-6

2. Revelation 5:9-10

Now let's look at Hebrews 5:1-3: "For every high priest taken from among men is appointed on behalf of men in things pertaining to God, in order to offer both gifts and sacrifices for sins; he can deal gently with the ignorant and misguided, since he himself also is beset with weakness; and because of it he is obligated to offer sacrifices for sins, as for the people, so also for himself."

The author of Hebrews is making a point about the Levitical priests. The Levitical priests were able to deal gently with those who sinned because they had sinned also. They were men with weaknesses just like those they represented.

Although Jesus never sinned, He was tempted in all points as we are. Therefore, He can sympathize with our weaknesses. We can come to Him and know that He understands.

And when you have experienced hurt, you can understand the hurts and rejections others have experienced. And when you have found healing from the balm of Gilead, you can share with them what God has done for you! You become God's "priest" to a hurting world, giving them a message of hope and encouragement! I have seen this very thing in my own life.

It is in the light of how God uses our past to minister to others that I want to share the following letter.

I want to thank you for your personal testimony. And to thank God for giving you the grace to be transparent and so vulnerable. I hope I can express in words how God used your witness to help me feel a part of the Body of Christ.

I, too, have an immoral past and will be eternally grateful for the saving blood of Jesus. But I had a problem with my new family (Christians). I felt uncomfortable and unworthy to serve Him. I wasn't sure of just how to fit in, or even if I ever could find my place. Most of the time I felt like the tainted woman trying to be part of the vestal virgins.

But Jesus released me through you. For I looked at you and saw myself. At last, there was someone just like me. My heart jumped inside of me! I wanted to shout it out! If God could do for you as He has, then He has a place for me also.

My heart is being cleansed and my mind renewed through what I am learning in the Word through Precept Bible Studies. For the first time in my Christian life, I am being transformed from the inside out. Praise God.

Beloved, if you will believe God and obey Him, He will redeem your past and use it for the glory of His kingdom!

— D A Y   T H R E E —

I have another reason for sharing my friend's letter.

Did you notice what she said about her heart being cleansed and her mind being renewed through studying God's Word? Being in the Word of

God is absolutely essential to your healing. Many are not being healed because they have run to drink the polluted waters of Egypt's Nile, the world's wisdom, instead of turning to the fountain of living waters, Jesus Christ, and to the Word of God.

Sin, whether committed by us or committed against us, mars and scars the image of God. Restoration to that beautiful image of Christlikeness comes as we are transformed by the Word of God. I have seen it in my life and in the lives of countless others.

Write out Romans 12:1-2. Read the words aloud until you have memorized them.

To understand Romans 12:1-2 you must know the context. Paul is urging his readers to present their bodies as living sacrifices in light of the truths of Romans chapters 1–11. Scholars feel that the living sacrifice parallels the burnt offering mentioned in Leviticus 1. A burnt offering was a voluntary offering, totally given to God and consumed on the altar. It all belonged to God. Nothing was given to the priests, as was the case with some of the other sacrifices.

With the word *therefore* in Romans 12:1, God makes His appeal on the basis of what He has done to set you free from sin's penalty and power.

Now He asks: Will you present yourself to Me to be totally Mine, set apart for Me and for My purpose?

If God were to say that to you today, how would you respond? Why? Write it out below.

— *D A Y   F O U R* —

Some people are afraid to give themselves to God for fear that He might send them to Africa. I don't know why it is always Africa, but it is!

Others are afraid that God might keep them single all their lives. Some fear that because they're divorced God won't let them get married again.

Others are afraid to give themselves totally to God because He might bring sickness or tragedy to their lives or to the lives of their loved ones.

Still others are afraid that God might want them to be reconciled to those they do not want to love or to forgive.

Some believe surrender to God might keep them from the happiness they desperately crave. God might not allow them to be what they want to be, to do what they want to do, to have what they want to have.

From all that you have learned so far, my friend, do you think these fears are valid? What would you tell someone who had these fears? Write out what you would say. As much as possible, use the Word of God in your answer.

Were any of these fears yours? Can you accept the answer you just gave?

— D A Y   F I V E —

Healing begins with trust.

If you do not trust God, then you can't take Him at His Word. And if you can't take Him at His Word, then you are refusing the only certain means of healing.

Where else, my friend, will you find a sure cure for your hurts? If the God who made you and who has set His love on you can't heal you, how can mere man?

O Beloved, if you have not already done so, as much as you know how, will you present yourself to God now, without restraint? If so, write out your commitment and personalize it by using "I."

As I said, healing begins with trust. Trust comes from knowing God's Word. The Word is God's tool to transform us. All of which leads to Romans 12:2 where God tells us: "And do not be conformed to this world, but be transformed by the renewing of your mind, that you may prove what the will of God is, that which is good and acceptable and perfect."

The battleground for our healing is the mind, our thought life. We are going to look at that in depth next week, so be patient. We have to learn one principle at a time.

Write out Matthew 15:18-20. Let me remind you that to the Jew, the mind and the heart were the same. So, when you write *heart*, think *mind.*

Can you see why God says, "Do not be conformed to this world, but be transformed by the renewing of your mind, that you may prove what the will of God is, that which is good and acceptable and perfect" (Romans 12:2)? If it is our minds that defile us or are the source of our actions and responses, it is vital that our minds be renewed. Proverbs 4:23 says, "Keep thy heart with all diligence; for out of it are the issues of life" (KJV).

You live according to your beliefs. When I say beliefs, I don't mean knowledge. Knowledge is only a portion of belief. Genuine belief is active. It lives according to the knowledge it has.

The Christian life is to be a whole new way of thinking. And that is where healing comes. When you know God's Word, you gain a new perspective on pain and suffering—God's perspective. You see why you can give thanks in everything, for you have God's mind, not man's. This brings healing.

As you submit to God, placing your all on the altar, and as you are transformed by the renewing of your mind, then, precious friend, you will know the will of God. You will find it acceptable, good, and perfect.

— D A Y   S I X —

A renewed mind will enable you to deal with your past by giving you a different perspective.

When your past torments you, when the father of lies whispers what-might-have-been-if-only, a renewed mind will counterattack with the truth of Romans 8:28-30. A renewed mind will hold fast to the promise that all will work together for good.

Now then, let's look at 2 Corinthians 5:14-21.

1. As you read through the text, mark every reference to *Jesus Christ* with the same distinctive mark (e.g., draw a cross) or color. Then in the right-hand margin, list everything you learn about Jesus Christ from these verses.

2. Mark each reference to *us* in a distinctive way. Also mark any reference to the believer in the same way you mark *us: all, they, themselves, we, man.* Then at the end of the passage, make a list of what you learn about you as a believer.

▶ 2 CORINTHIANS 5:14-21

14 For the love of Christ controls us, having concluded this, that one died for all, therefore all died;

15 and He died for all, that they who live should no longer live for themselves, but for Him who died and rose again on their behalf.

16 Therefore from now on we recognize no man according to the flesh; even though we have known Christ according to the flesh, yet now we know Him thus no longer.

17 Therefore if any man is in Christ, he is a new creature; the old things passed away; behold, new things have come.

18 Now all these things are from God, who reconciled us to Himself through Christ, and gave us the ministry of reconciliation,

19 namely, that God was in Christ reconciling the world to Himself, not counting their trespasses against them, and He has committed to us the word of reconciliation.

20 Therefore, we are ambassadors for Christ,

as though God were entreating through us; we beg you on behalf of Christ, be reconciled to God.

21 He made Him who knew no sin to be sin on our behalf, that we might become the righteousness of God in Him.

New creatures—what a promise to those who hurt! I love you, Beloved.

— D A Y   S E V E N —

Second Corinthians 5:14-21 states a number of wonderful absolutes about the child of God. Absolutes are fixed and immutable (unchangeable) qualities, concepts, or standards. One of the absolutes is the fact that Christ died for all, and that, therefore, you died. This is the same truth or absolute which we saw in our study of Romans 6.

When Jesus Christ died, God caused us to die with Him. This means that our *old man* died—all that we were through the first Adam before we came to believe in our Lord Jesus Christ. In the mind and heart of God, the old you no longer exists. Paul expresses this truth in Galatians 2:20. Write this verse out in the space provided.

1. What do you see in 2 Corinthians 5:17...
   a. about every child of God?

   b. about what has passed away?

2. What makes you a new creature, besides the fact that old things have passed away? Or to put it another way, what makes us different from people in the world who have not been genuinely saved? Read Romans 8:9. Write out the verse and the answer to this question.

3. Now, thinking of all this information and the other truths you have seen in our study, fill in the diagram I have drawn for you. Record the dates of the following events on the appropriate place on the chart.
   a. Note when God chose you for Himself.
   b. Enter the date when you were physically born (the crib symbolizes that).
   c. Put the date of your salvation above the stick figure with the cross. If you do not know the date, that's fine. Just approximate. If you feel that you received Jesus as Savior at an early age but did not have a changed life until you made Him Lord, why don't you put down the latter date?

d. In the appropriate place, put where old things passed away and all things became new.

e. On the chart indicate your hurts in the time frame when they occurred by putting an X for each hurt. Note all of your hurts, whether they resulted from your own sins or from the sins of others. When did most of them happen to you? Write out your answer.

If your hurts occurred before you came to know Jesus Christ, then they belong to a person who died.

In 2 Corinthians 5:16 God says, "Therefore from now on we recognize no man according to the flesh; even though we have known Christ according to the flesh, yet now we know Him thus no longer."

God is saying that once a person dies through identification with Jesus Christ he or she becomes a new creature. Therefore, we don't point to what the person was in the past. It's gone! That person, as he or she was, no longer exists.

Stop and meditate on this, Beloved. Are you living shackled to a corpse? Are you living in the light of your past, or are you living in the light of all Jesus Christ has accomplished for you at Calvary?

You may answer, "But I can't forget what has been said and done to me. I can't forget my past and all of my failures. They haunt me."

Tomorrow and in our next week of study, you are going to learn how to deal moment by moment with the thoughts which torment you.

Or you may say to me, "But, Kay, it is what I did after I came to know the Lord Jesus Christ that is tormenting me! How could I ever do that to my Lord? I wish it had happened before I knew Him, but it didn't. Now what do I do?"

You must run to 1 John 1:9, do what it says, and believe God will do what He says that He will do.

Today, I want you to meditate on what you have learned in 2 Corinthians 5. Remember your focus is to be on Christ and who you are in Christ, not on what you were before you met Him.

MEMORY VERSE

Therefore if any man is in Christ, he is a new creature; the old things passed away; behold, new things have come.

2 CORINTHIANS 5:17

SMALL-GROUP DISCUSSION QUESTIONS

In week seven we learned that God truly was and is in control of our individual lives. We know from Psalm 139 that He knew us as we were being formed in our mother's womb and that He has watched over us every day, every moment of our lives, allowing things that He could use to conform us into the image of His Son.

We saw that our past, our hurts, etc. were not mistakes and that we could be thankful for all that has happened because as we yield to Him, He will use it in our lives.

We learned too that we need to be persistent in our prayers for our healing, but we also need to be willing to receive His answer to our prayers, realizing that because we are His children and because of His great love for us that His answer will be good—good for us.

1. In your study in Revelation, how did you see God refer to believers?

2. What was the point that was made in Hebrews 5:1-3 about the Levitical priests? What did you see earlier about your High Priest that goes along with this fact about the Levitical priests? What does this mean for you?

3. What is Paul calling you to do in Romans 12:1-2? What did this offering parallel? What is the significance of this truth?

4. What is the tool that God will use to transform us?

5. As you studied Romans 12:1-2, what did you see that needed to be renewed?

6. From your study, what is it that defiles a man?

7. What can you do to see that your mind, your thoughts, do not defile you?

8. What did you learn in 2 Corinthians 5 about every believer?

9. From 2 Corinthians 5, what did you see had passed away? What assures you that you are a new person? What do you possess that others in the world do not have?

10. In light of your study this week, what do you think is true about your past?

11. Are you living in the light of your past instead of in the light of what Jesus has provided for you? If so, why? What do you plan to do in light of this week's study?

12. What do you think 2 Corinthians 5:16 means in respect to you?

YOUR MIND: THE BATTLEFIELD

— D A Y   O N E —

If you have been wounded through verbal, emotional, or physical abuse, you are in a warfare for your life. (Not necessarily for your physical life, unless you are contemplating suicide or your health has been affected by bitterness.) Your spiritual life is under siege.

Satan will fight long and hard to hold a soul in his dominion of darkness (Acts 26:18). However, when the Spirit begins the process of bringing God's lost sheep to salvation, Satan must let them go.

Satan's power over a soul is broken because sin has been completely paid for by the blood of Jesus Christ. However, salvation does not end a person's battle with the forces of the evil one. Satan desires to sift us as wheat, to make us weak and ineffectual servants in the kingdom of God. Having lost us to God, he knows that we are God's forever, yet the reality of that truth does not stop him from attacking us.

And where does the enemy attack first? If you answered, "In our minds or in our thoughts," you are so right! As we have seen, evil comes from the mind, the heart. "As [a man] thinks within himself, so he is" (Proverbs 23:7). This is why in Proverbs we read, "Watch over your heart with all diligence, for from it flow the springs of life" (4:23).

Satan wants to fill your mind with thinking that is contrary to God's Word. Write out John 8:44 and memorize it.

Satan would tell you that because of what has been done to you, you can never be whole, well, healed, set free, or of any value to God. *That is a lie!* Any thought that takes you back to your life before Christ and torments you is not from God. God always looks at you as you are in Christ Jesus, a new creature.

Satan, however, wants you to focus on what you were. He hates it that you are now a new creature, and so he wages war on your thought life. If Satan can cause you to focus your thoughts on things which are past, then you cannot dwell or concentrate on what God has before you. This is why Paul wrote, "One thing I do: forgetting what lies behind and reaching forward to what lies ahead, I press on toward the goal for the prize of the upward call of God in Christ Jesus" (Philippians 3:13-14).

Read through 2 Corinthians 10:3-7. See what you can observe from this passage on your own. It is a treasure!

These words of Paul were written because of some slanderous and unkind remarks which were being made about him.

▶ 2 CORINTHIANS 10:3-7

3 For though we walk in the flesh, we do not war according to the flesh,

4 for the weapons of our warfare are not of the flesh, but divinely powerful for the destruction of fortresses ("strongholds," KJV).

5 We are destroying speculations ("imaginations," KJV) and every lofty thing raised up against the knowledge of God, and we are taking every thought captive to the obedience of Christ,

6 and we are ready to punish all disobedience, whenever your obedience is complete.

7 You are looking at things as they are outwardly. If anyone is confident in himself that he is Christ's, let him consider this again within himself, that just as he is Christ's, so also are we.

1. Now mark every use of the pronoun *we*, and then record everything you learn about it.

2. Record what these verses tell us about...
   a. our warfare

   b. our weapons

3. According to verse 7, what were the Corinthians doing that they shouldn't have been doing? Can you see any parallel between what you see in verse 7 and what 2 Corinthians 5:16 is saying? Explain.

4. Begin memorizing 2 Corinthians 10:3-5. Again I suggest reading it aloud three times each morning, noon, and night until you can say it from memory.

— D A Y   T W O —

Before we look at 2 Corinthians 10:3-7, let me give you the context. It will encourage you to know that Paul understands your hurt. I also want you to see how God used Paul's hurt as a means of ministering to us so that we can learn from his experience.

As awesome as Paul seems to us, not all those he met and ministered among appreciated him. Some turned against him. Can you imagine the hurt that brings? I have had it happen to me. The pain is real.

It's obvious that some in Corinth were looking down on Paul because of his appearance. If God did not make you what the world considers normal or beautiful, I'm sure you can relate. When I was a child, I was teased because I was so skinny—they called me "Toothpick," "Broomstick." I didn't have curve one when other girls got theirs, and in those days curves were more in than bones!

Paul was unimpressive. In verse 10 we read, "His letters are weighty and strong, but his personal presence is unimpressive, and his speech contemptible." Tradition tells us that Paul was short, bow-legged, small. We are also told that he had an eye disease that was repulsive at times because of the yellow, crusty secretion that came from his eyes. Can you imagine how he could have felt, living in a society that literally worshiped beautiful

Greek physiques, that erected gorgeous statues of gorgeous bodies all over the place?

Some were saying that the only thing bold about Paul was his letters. Even his speech left a lot to be desired! Remember this society loved eloquence and rhetoric. They were caught up in worldly wisdom and all that went with it.

Through these people's tongues, the enemy was trying to destroy Paul's ministry. Plus, he was propelling his fiery darts straight at Paul's mind. If he could get Paul to focus his thoughts on these accusations and cutting remarks and to lash back at the Corinthians, Satan would win a great victory.

Paul knew his enemy. He was not ignorant of Satan's tricks, methods, or devices. That's why Paul reminds the Corinthians that although we walk in the flesh, although we live in a fleshly body, we don't war with fleshly means. Our warfare is not with flesh and blood!

Satan's goal is to set up strongholds or fortresses in our minds. Our responsibility is to stop him. In warfare it's strategic to set up a beachhead in your enemy's territory. This gives an inside base of operations. And as it is in earthly warfare between nations, so it is in spiritual warfare between Satan and his demonic host and God and His angelic host.

When you dwell on things that are not of God or that are against God, or when you fantasize evil, you are giving the enemy ground on which he can erect a stronghold or a fortress. This is why Paul says we are "destroying speculations (or imaginations) and every lofty thing raised up against the knowledge of God" (verse 5). If Paul had not destroyed the speculations, the imaginations, the thoughts that were contrary to the Word of God, they could have become the means of destroying him.

Paul goes on to say, "We are taking every thought captive to the obedience of Christ." In other words, whenever a thought came to Paul's mind, he evaluated it to see if it was pleasing to Christ and if it was in accord with the Word of God.

Now then, I have given you enough to meditate upon for today.

Write out what you have learned that you can personally apply to your life.

— *D A Y   T H R E E* —

When I teach 2 Corinthians 10:3-5, I use this drawing to explain my point:

Obviously, I'm not an artist!

If you will notice, I have Satan standing outside of the mind, knocking at the door. Of course our minds don't have doors. But this picture describes what Satan wants—access to our thoughts. He wants to focus our thoughts on things contrary to the truth about us as children of God, things contrary to the Word of God. Knowing that evil proceeds from the mind, he wants to bring lies or half-truths into our thoughts so that we might dwell on them. Because he's crafty, he is not going to knock at the door of my mind and say, "Hey, hey, hey, Kay baby, this is Satan. Say, how about you and me havin' a little chat?"

He's subtle. He never announces who he is unless you desire to talk to him. He can disguise himself as an angel of light or as one of your thoughts. He'll drop suggestions in your mind that can throw you for a loop if you don't know where they came from.

When I was about a year old in the Lord, I was invited to speak at a ladies' meeting at a local church. I had laced my testimony with the Word of God, and God had used it. I was so excited. I sang song after song to the Lord, making up the words as I drove home in my VW camper.

Suddenly in the midst of rejoicing in what the Lord had done, this thought came into my mind: *You did a wonderful job. You are a great speaker.* My joy screeched to a halt. *Those were prideful thoughts! God doesn't use proud people. He resists the proud. Now I can't speak anymore because I have pride!*

I was absolutely crushed. I didn't want to be proud. My joy was dead. For a while I was shaken. Then light began to dawn…*Those thoughts of pride were not my thoughts. That's not the way I feel about myself. God worked—it couldn't be me. I am simply His willing and excited and nervous vessel, filled by Him. Hmm, where did those thoughts come from then?*

I have the mind of Christ. That's what 1 Corinthians 2:16 says, and Christ would not think that kind of thoughts. They are not thoughts which belong to Him. Hmm, and they aren't thoughts I want to think. Oh, they are from the devil!

What release this understanding brought! I didn't have pride. I could be used by my Father!

Can you relate? Do you understand what I'm saying? Satan made me think those thoughts were my thoughts. But they weren't! They don't belong to the mind of Christ.

What thoughts are you thinking that do not belong to the mind of Jesus? How can you tell they don't belong to Him? We'll look at that tomorrow…unless, of course, you can't wait.

— D A Y   F O U R —

Every thought and feeling that you and I have must be brought captive to the obedience of Jesus Christ. Our thoughts must submit to the truths of the Word of God or be refused.

You need to walk in obedience to Philippians 4:8. The first thing I do with thoughts which come to the door of my mind is to frisk them. As I tell my students, when a thought comes knocking at the door of your mind, you "Philippians 4:8" it. By this I mean you need to examine each thought to see if it meets the conditions of Philippians 4:8.

Look up Philippians 4:8, and list the conditions the thought must meet.

IT MUST BE _____

_____

_____

_____

_____

How many of these conditions do you think a thought must meet? Write out your answer and why.

Now, Beloved, Philippians 4:8 it!

— D A Y   F I V E —

One of Satan's tactics is to make you feel rejected. Rejection hurts. It isolates. It's destructive.

I want us to look at rejection. Then when the enemy comes with all of his "rejection ammunition," you will know how to detonate it—in his face, not yours!

You can be certain that rejection comes in one form or another to every child of God. Suffering and persecution are a part of the life of those who belong to Jesus Christ. Remember Jesus suffered rejection from His own, for "He came unto his own, and his own received him not" (John 1:11, KJV). And He was perfect. There was no fault in Him. Yet, "He was despised, and we did not esteem Him" (Isaiah 53:3). Don't you think Jesus can understand and sympathize with your rejection?

So often I have thought, *If only I could have been perfect, then people wouldn't have rejected me.* I have groaned and wept over my own inadequacies, my own failures, my own stupidities, and I have thought, *If only I had...*or *If only I hadn't....* I think, *Why didn't I...? I should have...Why am I...?* Rejection hurts. I know. I understand.

All of my mail does not consist of love letters! Everyone who talks to me is not always pleased with me. Every member of my family does not love me or accept me the way I am. And try as I may, I'm not all I should be. I have to deal with rejection, some of which comes because of my personality and inadequacies and some because of the gospel.

How do I handle it?

By bringing my thoughts captive to Jesus Christ, by listening to God's Word, by believing it, and by walking in obedience to it.

By accepting that "by the grace of God I am what I am" (1 Corinthians 15:10) and by believing that I am in the process of being conformed into His image.

By trying to learn from my mistakes and seeking to turn from that which is not Christlike in character and behavior.

By remembering Paul's words and making them my own: "Brethren, I do not regard myself as having laid hold of it [Christlikeness] yet; but one thing I do: forgetting what lies behind and reaching forward to what lies ahead, I press on toward the goal for the prize of the upward call of God in Christ Jesus" (Philippians 3:13-14).

By remembering—

that my Lord, who was perfect, was rejected.

that even Jesus' half-brothers didn't believe on Him and, in essence, rejected Him (John 7:5).

that some people whom Paul had led to the Lord didn't like him and talked against him.

the experience of the prophets who were rejected by the people and even by priests and kings.

I am God's bondservant and not man's, "For am I now seeking the favor of men, or of God? Or am I striving to please men? If I were still trying to please men, I would not be a bond-servant of Christ" (Galatians 1:10).

I also handle rejection by clinging to the following scriptures, which I want you to look up. Write them out or record the main thought of each. Note how they apply to you.

The first two references explain the rejection which comes from the gospel.

1. Matthew 10:34-37

2. John 15:18-21

3. Psalm 27:7-10 (If you have the time, it would be profitable for you to look at the entire psalm.)

4. Hebrews 13:5-6 (I would memorize these verses, if I were you. What comfort they brought me when I memorized them soon after I was saved.)

God will *not* leave us nor forsake us. We are accepted in the Beloved. "Having predestinated us unto the adoption of children by Jesus Christ to himself...he hath made us accepted in the beloved" (Ephesians 1:5-6, KJV).

Others may—will—reject you. God never guarantees that they won't. They may reject you because of your Christianity. But it is because you belong to Christ that God has engraved you on the palms of His hands through the covenant of grace.

But Zion said, "The LORD has forsaken me, and the Lord has forgotten me." "Can a woman forget her nursing child, and have no compassion on the son of her womb? Even these may forget, but I will not forget you. Behold, I have inscribed you on the palms of My hands." (Isaiah 49:14-16)[1]

There are times when you might think the Lord has forgotten you as His child—times when the pain, the hurt, and the rejection are so bad that you can hardly stand it. You need to run into the shelter of His Word. Behold your Savior. Put your finger in the nail prints. Remember that God has loved you with an everlasting love.

You are accepted in the Beloved. He will never, never, never leave you or forsake you. God will not—*cannot*—reject His own.

"There is therefore now no condemnation for those who are in Christ Jesus.... Who shall separate us from the love of Christ? Shall tribulation, or distress, or persecution, or famine, or nakedness, or peril, or sword?" Did you think that these things were signs that God did not love you, that He had forsaken you? Were you depressed and despairing because you were enduring things such as these?

"It is written, 'FOR THY SAKE WE ARE BEING PUT TO DEATH ALL DAY LONG; WE WERE CONSIDERED AS SHEEP TO BE SLAUGH-TERED.' But in all these things we overwhelmingly conquer through Him who loved us. For I am convinced that neither death, nor life, nor angels, nor principalities, nor things present, nor things to come, nor powers, nor height, nor depth, nor any other created thing, shall be able to separate us from the love of God, which is in Christ Jesus our Lord." (Romans 8:1,35-39)

— D A Y   S I X —

As you know, my past was not a pretty one. It was filled with sin and its awful harvest. After I was saved, at times I would find my mind roaming back into my past. I didn't always know what stimulated the thoughts. Sometimes they were triggered by circumstances of life, the seeing of some scene, the hearing of certain music. But often they just popped into my mind. When I entertained these thoughts, many times I would find depression setting in as I questioned why I had done what I had or as I simply rehearsed the past. Often during these times, I would dwell on my mistakes, my failures, my weaknesses, my sins, my…

Thoughts not under control lead to depression. To be depressed is to be "pressed down." If the cause of your depression is not physical or biochemical, it could be that you are depressed because you are dwelling on your past or because you are angry with God or with man. Depression can come when we allow our circumstances to overwhelm us, throwing us into a state of mental or physical inertia. Depression can also be a symptom of unbelief.

Although we cannot study the subject of depression, I want us to look at how we can deal with thoughts of the past which cause constant pain and lead to depression. Reason with me from the Word. Everything that you did before you were saved is not true of the new you.

Was your past one of alcoholism, lesbianism, homosexuality, murder, adultery, fornication, abortion, perversion, lying, stealing, cursing, brutality? When you did what you did, you did it under the dominion of the "old man." 1 Corinthians 6:9-11 says, "Do not be deceived; neither fornicators, nor idolaters, nor adulterers, nor effeminate, nor homosexuals, nor thieves, nor the covetous, nor drunkards, nor revilers, nor swindlers, shall inherit the kingdom of God. And such *were* some of you; but you *were washed,* but you *were sanctified,* but you *were justified* in the name of the Lord Jesus Christ, and in the Spirit of our God" (italics mine).

Before you were saved, were you molested, abused, demeaned, rejected? That person died with Christ (Romans 6:6). Everything that happened to you before you came to know Jesus Christ belongs to a dead man or woman. Why are you trying to resurrect that person? Why are you chaining your thoughts to a corpse? Dead bodies rot and smell!

Have you ever had a dead mouse in your house? I have—several as a matter of fact. The exterminator told us the mice would eat the poison, get thirsty, and head to the creek for water. Some of them must have eaten too much poison. They never got to the water. They never left the house! The stench was sickening.

The stench of your old man can be overwhelming, sickening. Keep the nails on the coffin. Don't sit on the old man's tombstone and reminisce or weep about your past. That behavior is not what God wants.

When your thoughts want to wander over the past, go to God in prayer, saying something like this:

O Father, I am so thankful that that person no longer lives; that part of me is dead, never to be resurrected. Thank You that those old things have passed away. Thank You for making me new, brand-new. Thank You for forgiving all my sins, for remembering them no more, for putting them behind Your back, for removing them as far as the east is from the west. O Father, forgive me for even beginning to remember, to recall what You have so adequately taken care of, forgiven, and forgotten. Lord, I will focus my thoughts on those things that You say are true of me now.

Now then, Beloved, what from your past is depressing you? Put it away in a prayer of faith. Write out your prayer, then read it aloud.

I wonder if some of you are thinking, *Wait a minute! Don't leave me here! You talked about the things of my 'B.C.' days being buried with my old man, but what if they have been done to my new man? What if they have happened since I came to know Jesus Christ?*

Good question. What has happened to the "new man" will be discussed as we look at how to deal with anger, unforgiveness, and bitterness in the remaining chapters of this book.

– D A Y   S E V E N –

There are two psalms which will help you deal with thoughts of rejection and things which can cause depression.

Using your Bible, read through Psalms 42 and 43 carefully. As you do, mark the following words in a distinctive way: *God* (and all the appropriate pronouns referring to God), *soul, despair, disturbed, rejected,* and *hope.*

When you have finished, list everything you learned from each word.

God:

Soul:

Despair:

Disturbed:

Rejected:

Hope:

Your soul is your inner man: the mind, the will, the emotions—what makes you "you." In order to help clarify what you observed in marking and listing each use of the word *soul* in Psalms 42 and 43, let me ask you some questions.

1. Why was the psalmist's soul panting and thirsting for God?

2. Have you ever experienced something similar? What was the occasion of such a panting and thirsting on your part?

3. What is the psalmist dealing with in his relationship to God?

4. Have you ever felt this way about God and your relationship to Him, or His relationship to you? When? Why?

5. Despair is a lack of hope. What do you learn about despair and its cure in these psalms?

6. Can you see any specific actions from the psalmist's experience which you can follow when you are in despair and feel rejected by God?

If you will pray these psalms back to God, you will find their truths taking root in your heart and bringing forth hope.

Let me give you an example of what I mean by praying back scripture to the Lord. Take the scripture verse by verse, or thought by thought, and personalize it for yourself or for others. For example, in my quiet time this morning as I read Psalm 9, I felt led to get on my knees and pray back that psalm to the Lord on behalf of all of my brothers and sisters who are suffering for the gospel of Jesus Christ. As I did, I personalized it for their situation. I also found myself praying for those of you who are taking this course and who are so afflicted by others.

The psalms are especially wonderful to turn into prayers, for they are the outpourings and musings of the heart. Let me show you how I do it by using the first five verses of Psalm 42.

Maybe you are hurting over your daughter. Then the prayer might go like this:

O Father, my heart is panting for You just as the deer pants for the water brook. I am hurting, God, and people are saying that You have deserted me. In my trials, they are asking where You are and why You are allowing me to go through what I am going through.

O God, I want to pour out my heart, my soul, to You. Help me in this despair to stop and remember the joy that I have known with You in the past, how I led others with the voice of joy and thanksgiving.

O Father, I am in despair because I am hurting. You know the pain that I have endured because my daughter wants nothing to do with You. You know that I feel I have failed in being all that I should have been. But, O Lord, You are greater than all my failures. You can help me in this situation.

That is how I personalize and pray back scripture to God. Why don't you try it, at least a verse or two, right now?

Throughout these psalms, the psalmist tells God exactly how he feels, but he does not stop there. He remembers and rehearses what God has done, who He is, and what He will do.

The psalmist looks at his past relationship with God. He recognizes that this time of despair will pass and that he will again praise God. He recognizes that if help is going to come, it is going to come from God.

As in the other psalms, once the heart and needs of the psalmist are laid before God along with the questions and doubts, peace is found in the act of trusting God.

O Beloved, if you are in despair, run to the psalms. Pray them back to God—aloud—until the sweet relief of faith comes.

MEMORY VERSE

For though we walk in the flesh, we do not war according to the flesh, for the weapons of our warfare are not of the flesh, but divinely powerful for the destruction of fortresses. We are destroying speculations and every lofty thing raised up against the knowledge of God, and we are taking every thought captive to the obedience of Christ.

2 CORINTHIANS 10:3-5

SMALL-GROUP DISCUSSION QUESTIONS

In week eight you looked at the fact that God has made you a priest, and you saw how He could use your past to open up a door of ministry for you. You are literally a new creature in Christ; old things have passed away.

You saw God calling you to become a living sacrifice and to renew your mind so that you can be used by God.

1. Now that you are a new creation in Christ and now that your "old man" is dead, who is your enemy?

2. Where does the enemy usually attack a believer? What are some of the feelings, thoughts, and emotions which resulted from our past—or from a present situation—that we must now deal with?

3. What did you learn in John 8:44 about your enemy? What does this fact let you know about him and the way he will come against you?

4. What did you learn in 2 Corinthians 10:3-6 about your weapons in your warfare with the enemy?

5. What is your primary weapon against the lies of the enemy?

6. What are you to do with thoughts that come into your mind according to 2 Corinthians 10?

7. How can you bring every thought captive?

8. What particular scripture acts as a plumb line by which you can measure your thoughts to see that they are pleasing to God? What did you learn in this verse that your thoughts should be like?

9. Feelings of rejection are one of the main tactics of the enemy. What did you learn about how to handle these feelings?

10. How can you deal with feelings of depression that come as a result of your past?

11. What did you learn in Psalm 42 and Psalm 43 about how the psalmist dealt with his despair and feelings of rejection by God that you can apply to your life when you have similar feelings?

12. Has this week's lesson helped you in understanding that you can stand against the enemy's attacks on your mind and that you can think on the things which are pleasing to God? How do you plan to put into action what you have learned?

THE BATTLE'S ON!

— D A Y   O N E —

What do you do when the thoughts just won't go away? Remember, you are in a war. Satan's strategy is to besiege your mind until he wears down your resistance and captures your thoughts. You can expect a barrage of thoughts to be constantly hammering away at your defenses. It is spiritual warfare.

You can rejoice because Jesus is victor. Victory is assured as long as you let Him be your captain and do what He says. "Submit therefore to God. Resist the devil and he will flee from you" (James 4:7).

Now let's get down to the practical outworking of resisting the devil. You will find great help and insight into handling those persistent, wearying thoughts as we look at how Jesus dealt with Satan when He was tempted. Let's look at the account as recorded for us in Matthew.

As you read this passage, mark every reference to *Jesus* and to the *devil*. Make sure you also mark the pronouns so that you can tell whether they refer to our Lord or to the devil.

❶ MATTHEW 4:1-11

1 Then Jesus was led up by the Spirit into the wilderness to be tempted by the devil.

2 And after He had fasted forty days and forty nights, He then became hungry.

3 And the tempter came and said to Him, "If You are the Son of God, command that these stones become bread."

4 But He answered and said, "It is written, 'MAN SHALL NOT LIVE ON BREAD ALONE, BUT ON EVERY WORD THAT PROCEEDS OUT OF THE MOUTH OF GOD.'"

5 Then the devil took Him into the holy city; and he had Him stand on the pinnacle of the temple,

6 and said to Him, "If You are the Son of God throw Yourself down; for it is written, 'HE WILL GIVE HIS ANGELS CHARGE CONCERNING YOU'; AND 'ON their HANDS THEY WILL BEAR YOU UP, LEST YOU STRIKE YOUR FOOT AGAINST A STONE.'"

7 Jesus said to him, "On the other hand, it is written, 'YOU SHALL NOT PUT THE LORD YOUR GOD TO THE TEST.'"

8 Again, the devil took Him to a very high mountain, and showed Him all the kingdoms of the world, and their glory;

9 and he said to Him, "All these things will I give You, if You fall down and worship me."

10 Then Jesus said to him, "Begone, Satan! For it is written, 'YOU SHALL WORSHIP THE LORD YOUR GOD, AND SERVE HIM ONLY.'"

11 Then the devil left Him; and behold, angels came and began to minister to Him.

1. List what you learn about Satan's tactics in this passage.

2. In what area(s) did the devil tempt Jesus?

3. Can you see any parallels between the devil's temptation of Jesus and his temptation of you? Explain your answer.

4. How did the Lord Jesus Christ handle Satan's temptation?

Satan persisted in his attempt to seduce Jesus into sin. What a lesson there is for you and me in all of this! Satan refused to give up in his attempt to wear Jesus down. We must never give in to the enemy. We are to resist him over and over and over again, rejecting thought after thought that is not pleasing to God or that is not in accord with the Word of God. Everything the enemy says must be brought to the standard of God's plumb line. We are not to allow the enemy to take Scripture out of context or to twist and pervert it. Like Jesus, we are to resist the devil. We have that authority because of who is in us: "Greater is He who is in you than he who is in the world" (1 John 4:4).

When I deal with recurring thoughts which are contrary to Philippians 4:8, I command the enemy to depart from me in the name of the Lord Jesus Christ. Usually I say this aloud. If that is not appropriate, I say it under my breath. I will say something like this: "Satan, those thoughts are not from God. You have no place in me. Therefore, in the name of Jesus Christ and by the blood of Jesus Christ, I command you to leave me alone." Why address Satan? Jesus did. He rebuked him and told him to leave.

If you are not having victory in stopping persistent evil or demoralizing thoughts, then verbally address Satan in the way I've told you to. Claim the blood of Jesus Christ which defeated Satan. Memorize this verse: "And they overcame him because of the blood of the Lamb and because of the word of their testimony, and they did not love their life even to death" (Revelation 12:11).

Now, when you resist the devil, you may find him coming back with a second round of fire, then a third, and a fourth. You must continue to hold your ground in faithful obedience. Eventually this will stop.

Let's finish today's study by summarizing the truths you can apply when the devil comes around as a roaring lion, trying to devour your faith (1 Peter 5:8). As you make your list, personalize what you have learned. For instance, you might write out your insight like this: "I learned that I must _____."

– D A Y   T W O –

Doubt about the reality of the devil and the warfare a Christian faces is removed when one opens the Word of God and allows it to speak for itself. Ephesians 6:10-20 clearly states that we are in a war. Read it carefully.

▶ EPHESIANS 6:10-20

10 Finally, be strong in the Lord, and in the strength of His might.

11 Put on the full armor of God, that you may be able to stand firm against the schemes of the devil.

12 For our struggle is not against flesh and blood, but against the rulers, against the powers, against the world forces of this darkness, against the spiritual forces of wickedness in the heavenly places.

13 Therefore, take up the full armor of God, that you may be able to resist in the evil day, and having done everything, to stand firm.

14 Stand firm therefore, HAVING GIRDED YOUR LOINS WITH TRUTH, and HAVING PUT ON THE BREASTPLATE OF RIGHTEOUSNESS,

15 and having shod YOUR FEET WITH THE PREPARATION OF THE GOSPEL OF PEACE;

16 in addition to all, taking up the shield of faith with which you will be able to extinguish all the flaming missiles of the evil one.

17 And take THE HELMET OF SALVATION, and the sword of the Spirit, which is the word of God.

18 With all prayer and petition pray at all times in the Spirit, and with this in view, be on the alert with all perseverance and petition for all the saints,

19 and pray on my behalf, that utterance may be given to me in the opening of my mouth, to make known with boldness the mystery of the gospel,

20 for which I am an ambassador in chains; that in proclaiming it I may speak boldly, as I ought to speak.

1. In the right-hand margin of the text, make a list of what our struggle is against.

2. In the space following or in the right-hand margin, list what God tells His children to do in this passage. You need not be specific regarding each piece of the armor. Just simply note as one of your points that we are to put on the whole armor.

3. Now list each part of the armor and write out a brief description of how each piece relates to you as a child of God.

4. How do you think the armor relates to the Christian's warfare for his or her mind?

5. The devil will do everything he can to keep you from turning to the Great Physician and from applying the healing balm of Gilead to your wounds. He wants you to focus on your hurts and be consumed with your pain so that your life will be ineffective for God.

Can you see how an understanding of Ephesians 6 might be used to heal your hurts? For instance, how could the armor of God be effective in the healing process? Be as specific as you can. Someday soon you'll use these insights as God uses you to help others.

Let me give you an example. We are first told to gird our loins with truth. This part of the armor is difficult to understand, so let me explain it to you and show you how to apply it to your life.

You might write: *I'm going to learn the truths of God's Word so I can walk without stumbling.* [In Bible times when a man wanted to go somewhere in a hurry or had a job to do, he pulled the back of his robe between his legs and tucked it into his belt so he wouldn't trip over it or be hindered in his work. "Gird your loins" can also be translated "put on the belt of truth." In this case, the analogy is to the Roman soldiers' armor. The belt held the armor in place. The soldier would hook his breastplate and his sheath for his sword to the belt.] *For me this means I am to wrap God's Word around me so it holds everything else in place.*

Beloved, pray Ephesians 6:10-20 back to God. Remember when we talked about praying scripture back to God and I showed you how, using Psalm 42 (on page 156). Personalize these verses in light of your feelings, your hurts, your needs. Pray aloud.

— D A Y   T H R E E —

Some hurt because they have a distorted view of God and, consequently, of themselves. They are, as my friend Karen wrote, "filled with painful feelings of guilt, self-hatred, fears and worthlessness…caught in a web of performance-oriented acceptance in relationships, including the relationship with Jesus Christ." Let me tell you a little bit about Karen.

Karen always seemed to have it together. A godly woman, she has ministered to many through her spiritual gift of exhortation. Little did I realize she was struggling to cling to the truths of God's Word she shared with others.

I have known Karen for many years, but I didn't know until several weeks ago that she was a victim of incest. It was then she told what a beautiful work of healing the Lord recently had performed in her life. We prayed that God would use her testimony to minister to you.

Under the direction of her pastor, Karen began keeping a journal of scriptures she could personalize. She said, "These were scriptures that would affirm who I am in Christ. I found this exercise to be very difficult because I always seemed drawn to that which exposed my shortcomings and failures and that which I felt condemned me."

Can you relate or do you know others who can?

As Karen searched the Word, she saw faulty self-concepts and problem areas in her thinking. She listed these:

- Fear and anxiety dominated my life.
- I felt worthless, inferior, and was extremely self-conscious and disgusted with myself.

- I felt rejection from peers, family, and friends.
- I felt intense guilt and shame for allowing the abuse to occur or for the pleasure which some of it gave me. I had also accepted money from my uncle.
- Having lost self-respect, I became compliant, accepting wrong from others as something I deserved.
- My anger was directed toward myself.
- I had become performance-oriented in my relationships, especially my relationship with God. I sought approval, but I felt I was far short of God's approval.
- Confidence before God and man was sadly lacking. I always felt inadequate and insecure.

She went on, "As I looked over the list, I became aware that *self and feelings ruled my life.* No wonder I was in such bondage."

God did a mighty work of healing in Karen's life. It did not come by teaching which directs us to focus on self—self-love, self-worth, self-acceptance, self-esteem, the power of positive thinking, or positive confession. It was self that she was in bondage to. Healing came by exposure to and obedient faith in the Word of God. It came by being strong in the Lord and in the strength of His might. It came as she put on the whole armor of God.

Tomorrow we'll look at some more insights Karen gave me. However, today, let me just give you a word of warning, greatly needed in Christendom today.

From the beginning Satan has cast doubt on the Word of God. He wants you to question, doubt, distort, alter, embellish, discredit, or ignore the Word of God, or to substitute alternatives for the Word of God. Disguised as an angel of light, he will do anything and everything he can to undermine God's Word—Satan will dilute it, add to it, adulterate it.

Remember, *the Word of God is all you need in order to be perfect, thor-*

oughly adequate for every work of life (2 Timothy 3:16-17). Everything con-
nected to the armor of God had something to do with the Word of God.

The devil's tactic is not only to cause you to doubt, ignore, and dis-
obey God's Word. It is also to get you to doubt God's love. To doubt
God's love is to doubt His character. Once the enemy casts doubt in your
mind on God's love, he cuts you off from the only true and sure source of
healing—your Jehovah-rapha and the Word of God.

My friend, be warned. Know your God. Know His Word. And live
accordingly.

— D A Y   F O U R —

Karen is a faithful student of the Word, but her healing didn't come until
she did two things. First she faced the fact that she was a victim of incest.
Then she began to appropriate and apply God's truths to her particular
need.

She wrote:

Gradually the Lord enabled me to find in His Word a truth to counter-
act the lies I'd been accustomed to hearing. God's view of me was so different from my own and from what I had perceived others to have of
me. I would personalize these scriptures by writing them in a notebook
and inserting my name. Then I would read them aloud and savor the
truth. I needed to do a study on the character and attributes of God. My
concept of God had been faulty, and I longed to grasp His unconditional
love and acceptance and to be free of the fear of His wrath.

I also began studying law and grace from Romans. Because I had
been so conditioned to performance, I had not fully laid hold of the
blessing of God's grace in my life. I would just weep with joy as this truth
unfolded! As I began to understand AND accept God's grace, praise
became a natural overflow of my heart. I would awaken in the night

with a praise song or Scripture on my heart. Most mornings I now awaken and begin to praise and thank God that He holds my life in the hollow of His hand. I can trust Him with any circumstance which I might face that day, knowing He will use it to mature me in Christ.

I did a Bible study on who I am in Christ. Aware of the danger of too much self-preoccupation, my goal was to know God's estimate of His child and to understand His true character. Second Corinthians 3:18 took on special meaning as I saw the Word as a mirror. When I looked into the Word, with an unveiled face (totally stripped bare), I could be transformed into His lovely image and reflect Him.

In all of this, Karen was girding her loins with truth, putting on the breastplate of His righteousness. Her feet had been shod with the preparation of the gospel of peace. She was learning where she stood with God and with Jesus Christ. The whole process of reading, writing out, personalizing, and savoring the truths of God's Word enabled Karen to take up the shield of faith with which she is able to extinguish the fiery darts of the enemy. She donned her helmet of salvation, renewing her mind, so that she evaluated everything according to the Word of Christ. In the process, she was honing the sword of the Spirit, the Word of God. This is the one and only offensive weapon she would ever need to win the war with the evil one.

Through this study you are learning to do the same. How I pray you will be a hearer and doer of the Word so that what you hear will profit you because it is being united with faith! (Hebrews 4:2).[1]

− D A Y   F I V E −

We're going to spend the next two days letting your mind meditate on Psalm 119. Read through Psalm 119:1-88 in your own Bible, and follow these instructions:

1. Mark every reference to the Word of God in the same color. The words which refer to the Word of God that you will want to mark are...

   a. word   e. testimonies
   b. precepts   f. statutes
   c. law   g. ordinances
   d. judgments

2. Also mark each of the following words in a distinctive way: *salvation*, *hope*, and each reference to *God*, including the pronoun *Thy*. I usually mark references to deity in yellow.

3. Mark every reference to the word *affliction* and its synonyms.

As you read, personalize those verses which are meaningful to you by turning them into a prayer. For example, when I read verse 38, I might pray:

Heavenly Father, I *do* want You to establish Your Word to me, Your servant. I want Your Word to renew my mind and produce reverence for You. I want to worship You as You deserve to be worshiped.

The psalmist says, "It is good for me that I was afflicted, that I may learn Thy statutes" (119:71). You might pray:

Lord, thank You for showing me that my afflictions have driven me to Your Word. Forgive me for not clinging in gut-level faith to what You say rather than how I feel. I am learning how to live by Your statutes, moment by moment. "This is my comfort in my affliction, that Thy word has revived me." (Psalm 119:50)

— D A Y   S I X —

"Those who love Thy law have *great peace*, and nothing causes them to stumble" (Psalm 119:165, italics mine). That is God's promise, and His Word is sure.

Read through the remainder of Psalm 119 today, marking it as you did yesterday. Meditate. Give the Lord time to speak. Personalize in prayer those verses which have special meaning to you. You might begin by praying with the psalmist, "Let my cry come before Thee, O LORD; give me understanding according to Thy Word" (verse 169).

Isn't it wonderful to see the keeping, sustaining, life-giving power of the Word of God in afflictions? May you delight in His Word so that you do not perish in your affliction (Psalm 119:92). Thank Him that His Word is a lamp to your feet, and a light to your path (verse 105). Rejoice that He will sustain you and uphold you according to His Word (verses 116-117).

When you finish reading Psalm 119, list below how this psalm has ministered to you personally.

– D A Y   S E V E N –

As you studied Psalm 119 and noted each use of the word *afflicted,* you saw that affliction causes us to turn to the statutes of God. Affliction also gives us a ministry.

The comfort you receive enables you to minister to others with the same comfort which you received from Him (2 Corinthians 1:3-5). Thus we come to a very important truth: Having received the Lord Jesus Christ as your Savior, your life has a purpose. God has planned good works for you to walk in. Therefore all that you have endured in your pain will not only be for your good but also for His glory as you make yourself available to minister to others by telling what you have learned.

Let me use Karen as an example. She wrote:

God has given me precious friends with whom I shared my deepest feelings and greatest fears. They were supportive and encouraging, and, when needed, they confronted me. They listened with a nonjudgmental heart and helped me see many false concepts that had found root in my thinking. They believed in me as they trusted God to heal my hurts. God used them as an extension of His love for me.

My objective in allowing you to use this material is that of ministering to hurting women. Since I am more open about what happened to me, I have uncovered many victims of such abuse.

The apostle Paul was well aware of the crucial ministry we have in one another's lives. Look up the following scriptures, and write out what you learn from them in respect to our ministry to one another. Note the various ways we are to minister. Also be sure you see why we are to minister.

1. Ephesians 6:18-19

2. Hebrews 10:24-25

3. Galatians 6:1

4. Galatians 6:2

5. 1 Thessalonians 5:14-15

6. Romans 12:10-11,15

7. 2 Corinthians 1:3-5

8. Write out Ephesians 4:15-16.

As you live the scriptures you have studied today and as you exercise your spiritual gifts,[2] you will find that your "proper working" will cause the body of Christ to grow and be built up in love. Being available to take others by the hand and help them live in the light of God's Word is a much needed and incredibly rewarding ministry. I know of no greater joy than that of being used of God in the life of another.

Is God using you? Are you willing to be open and vulnerable so that others will find you approachable? Are you usable? Remember, you cannot continue in sin and be used.

Once you have allowed God to heal you through His Word, you are ready to be used by God in the healing of others. You don't have to be a professional counselor to help. Don't fall into the trap of that kind of thinking.

You have the Word of God. In Psalm 119:24, we read, "Thy testimonies also are my delight; they are my counselors" or, to put it literally, "the men of my counsel."

You have the Holy Spirit. His ministry is to guide you into all truth, to bring to your remembrance the truths you have learned. God's truth sanctifies and sets people free. So, when you minister, ask the Holy Spirit to show you what truths the person needs.

Remember why Jesus was given to you. Isaiah 9:6 says: "For a child will be born to us, a son will be given to us; and the government will rest on His shoulders; and His name will be called Wonderful Counselor,

Mighty God, Eternal Father, Prince of Peace." Jesus is to govern our lives. He does this by being our counselor.

So you do have what you need to minister to others, don't you? Beloved, take a few minutes to talk to your Father. Make yourself available to Him to be used to minister to others—even if it's just being available to listen, to pray, or to encourage, reprove, or exhort from God's Word. Watch what God does!

MEMORY VERSE

Those who love Thy law have great peace, and nothing causes them to stumble.

PSALM 119:165

SMALL-GROUP DISCUSSION QUESTIONS

In week nine you learned that when the enemy attacks your mind with thoughts that are lies you can bring your thoughts up against the truth of the Word of God and choose to think on the things that measure up to the standard set for you in Philippians 4:8.

You also learned how to deal with specific feelings of rejection and despair.

1. Last week we saw that you have an enemy, Satan. Now we see that in this warfare there are other forces at his disposal to assist in his attack against believers. What did you learn about these forces this week?
2. What did you learn from the account of Satan's attack on the Lord Jesus after He had been in the wilderness for forty days and nights?
   a. What was significant about the timing of Satan's attack?
   b. Read the first verse of the passage again. Was God shocked by what happened to Jesus? What does this mean to you?
   c. What things did he offer Jesus? Were they things that would have filled a legitimate need?

d. How did he approach Jesus? What did he do with the Word of God?

e. Did he turn and go away after Jesus refused him the first time?

f. What did our Lord do to combat the attacks of Satan?

g. Can you see any parallels between this attack on Jesus and the way the enemy attacks you?

3. In 1 John 4:4 you saw your authority. What does this verse mean to you on a daily basis?

4. In Ephesians 6 you learned more about your warfare and how to deal with your enemy.

a. Where is our struggle?

b. What are you instructed to do in order to stand against the enemy?

c. After you have followed the instructions for resisting the devil, there is one more instruction. What is it?

d. We see that we have a responsibility to others too. What is that responsibility?

5. What is especially significant about the girdle of truth for us in this particular study?

6. What did you learn about the other pieces of the armor?

7. How can an understanding of Ephesians 6 be used to heal your hurts?

8. Warfare is affliction from the enemy. What did you learn in Psalm 119 about affliction?

9. What does the Word do in affliction? What was the cry of the psalmist in light of the affliction?

10. At the end of your lesson, you looked up scriptures that show your affliction could be used by God to minister to others. What were some of the things you saw in these verses? How do you plan to apply what you have learned?

HOW CAN I FORGIVE?

— D A Y   O N E —

D o you wish to get well?"

The question must have been as shocking as a bucket of ice water thrown on his head. It certainly brought him to his senses. There he was face to face with The Truth. There was no more hiding in his infirmity, no more solace in his pain, no more excuses for what he could have been, could have done, could have had if he had been well. Now he was looking at the One who could heal him.

Did he wish to get well?

For thirty-eight years he had been ill. He had spent his days among others who were infirm, sick, crippled. There were no demands on him because he was afflicted. The world owed him his living, their pity, because life had dealt him an evil blow.

Did he wish to get well? It was a valid question.

Of course, he knew how he could be made well. He had it all figured out. That's why he had stayed beside the pool of Bethesda all of those years waiting for an angel to come and stir the waters. He knew the only way to be healed was to get into those stirred-up waters before anyone else. He answered Jesus, "Sir, I have no man to put me into the pool when the water is stirred up, but while I am coming, another steps down before me" (John 5:7).

This man would be healed! But not in the way he had planned. Instead, he merely had to arise, take up his pallet, and walk.

Do *you* wish to get well? Don't let the question offend you. Please don't.

There are some who love their wounds, their hurts, their sickness. Why? There are various reasons.

Their pain brings attention and pity. They relish parading their hurts before others. They want people to take their side, despising those who have hurt them. There's a twisted comfort in seeing them be rejected, hurt. How would they get even with those who hurt them if they were healed? How could they continue to make them suffer?

Many nurse their hurts because their wounds are an excuse for their shortcomings and failures. Their mentality is *I am the way I am because of what I have suffered. You can't expect anything else!* Healing would take away their excuse for who they are. It would make them take responsibility to be what they should be.

Others don't want to be healed because they are angry with God. If God healed them, then they would feel an obligation to Him—to be what God wants them to be. They don't want that. They are wrapped up in themselves, and to relinquish self would be to lose control. If that's the case, they don't want to be healed.

Some are not sure they would know how to live if they were healed. They fear change. In a sense, there is a false "comfortableness" in their pain. They have lived and survived this long. Why change?

Still others are so angry, bitter, despairing, demoralized, numb that it's hard to believe things could ever change. To them healing is not even an option—not probable, not possible. They don't realize they could be unshackled from the chains of bitterness and anger. There's hope for the despairing, the demoralized.

Having said all this, let's get back to the question at hand: Do you wish to get well? If your answer is yes, then I must ask you, Are you willing to get well on God's terms? Will you be made whole? Will you be healed no matter what God says to do? Or do you want to be healed only if you can do it your way and on your terms?

There is no wound too great, too deep, too damaging that it cannot be healed by the Spirit of God working through His Word. Healing is for those who will trust and obey.

In these final weeks of study, we are going to look at some specifics regarding forgiveness, anger, bitterness, love, and acceptance—essentials which must be dealt with if we are going to be healed. You may find yourself face to face with some difficult decisions regarding forgiving others, putting away anger and bitterness, acting in love, and accepting people who you feel owe you a debt which they have never paid.

You are going to find the Spirit of God asking again and again, Do you wish to get well? How I pray that your answer will be, "Yes, heal me, O Lord. I want to be healed, to be healthy and whole, so that I might serve You fully."

What are your hesitations, your fears, your questions when confronted with the question, Do you wish to get well? Write them out so that you can look back and see how God deals with them to effect your healing.

Physical wounds infected or filled with debris will never heal properly. The wounds must be thoroughly cleansed. The same principle applies to the spiritual and emotional realm of man's inner being. Healing doesn't come by ignoring the infection or debris or by slapping a bandage over the wound and waiting for it to be healed.

You can't cover the infection of hurt or the hot inflammation of the soul's pain and expect to get well. The wound must be discovered, opened, debrided, and cleansed thoroughly. Then healing can come. I'm not saying that you need to uncover things which the Lord has blotted out, those which you don't remember.

Rather whatever has been buried, stuffed down, or denied needs to be exposed so that the healing balm of Gilead can be applied and bring healing. You need not go digging around in your past using various unbiblical methods. In fact, Paul discourages rummaging around in the attic of your past: "Forgetting those things which are behind [past]" (Philippians 3:13, KJV).

If you have buried something that needs to be dealt with, then God will bring it to your mind as you pray, "Search me, O God...and see if there be any hurtful way [or way of pain] in me" (Psalm 139:23-24).

Healing is a process. It comes moment by moment, thought by thought, as you choose to believe God and to walk in obedience no matter how you feel. Did you notice the word *choose?*

Healing comes as you make the choice of believing, obeying, and clinging to the character of God and the Word of God. If you will cling to God as the waistband clings to the waist of a man, then God will make you a person "for renown, for praise, and for glory" (Jeremiah 13:1-11).

Let's begin the healing process by identifying the source of your wound. What do you think is causing you to hurt? Are you hurting because of something someone has done to you? Are you hurting because of something you have done to others or to God? Are you hurting because you are disappointed or angry at God because you think He has failed you?

Write out what you think God is showing you as the source of your hurts. Sometimes that is especially difficult to do because we do not want anyone to know about it. We fear that they will be disgusted with us or that they may reject us if they know what we have been involved in. Beloved, if God is for you, who can be against you? If God has not rejected you, then what right has man to do so? None. Man is not greater than God.

Remember the promise of Jeremiah 29:11. Look it up and write it out before you list your wounds and their sources.

Telling others why we hurt is often the means God uses for our healing. This is where the body of Christ comes in as God instructs us to bear one another's burdens (Galatians 6:2). I have been amazed at what happens when we follow the instructions given to us in James 5:16: "Confess your sins to one another, and pray for one another, so that you may be healed." Truly, the effective prayer of a righteous man availeth much.

Many people have written to me saying, "I have never told this to anyone before in my life, but..." In the very expression of their burden there has been a release just by letting another person whom they trust know what they have been involved in, endured, suffered.

A woman wrote me after I did a television series on incest. She was in her sixties, married for the third time, and hurting in such a way that it had affected her relationships with her family. She had been sexually molested by her father and her brothers. She was so afraid that if people found out about it they would think she was the cause. For almost fifty years that precious woman had been suffering needless pain, shame, and guilt...when all the time there was a balm of Gilead. Yet, she didn't discover the source of healing until she wrote for help.

I know people who have been victims of all sorts of perversion, even bestiality. I also know many who have been involved in lesbianism, homosexuality, or adultery. Absolutely sickened over it, they now doubt how God could ever use them. I know others who have victimized people in all sorts of twisted ways. They find it difficult to believe that God could ever forgive them, let alone use them. The exposing of these things to a mature Christian steeped in God's Word has brought release and victory.

If you can't express your hurt because of the pain of even mentioning it, it is a very real and infected wound. It must be lanced, opened, cleaned out, and treated with the balm of Gilead so that it can be healed.

Thank God today that there is no wound beyond His healing power! Thank Him too that His heart is for you and those you love to be healed!

— D A Y   T W O —

In preparation for the coming weeks of study on forgiveness, anger, bitterness, meekness, and rejection, I want to make sure you see that everything you have endured, suffered, or experienced can have eternal value if you will view it from God's perspective.

If there is any man in the Word of God who demonstrates this truth, it is Joseph. To see how he demonstrates this precept of life, you are going to have to do some reading in Genesis. It will take time, but it will be beneficial.

1. Genesis 37:1-36: Summarize below what you read about the rejection Joseph suffered from his brothers.

2. Genesis 39:1-23: Note the temptation and what Joseph suffered even in his innocence. Write out how Joseph was tempted and what he suffered as a result of his obedience to God. How long did it last? What was his response?

3. Genesis 40:1-23: Although Joseph didn't know it, God was ordering circumstances that would eventually bring about his deliverance. The same is true of you, and you can rest in this truth because of 1 Corinthians 10:13: "No temptation [trial or testing] has overtaken you but such as is common to man; and God is faithful, who will not allow you to be tempted [tried or tested] beyond what you are able, but with the temptation [trial or testing] will provide the way of escape also, that you may be able to endure it."

4. Genesis 41:1-57: When Pharaoh heard Joseph's interpretation of the dream, Pharaoh's heart was inclined toward Joseph. Joseph was thus moved into the position which eventually allowed him to use all that he had suffered for the benefit of his father and family and for Egypt.

    Because of the famine, Joseph's brothers went to Egypt to buy grain. Through a set of God-ordained circumstances, Joseph helped them by providing grain. He eventually revealed himself to his brothers. Read Chapters 42–44, if you have time.

5. Genesis 45:1-5: Write out verse 5. Also read Genesis 50:15-21. Write out verse 20 and note the words "this present result." Write out how these verses could be applied to you and your hurts.

This, Beloved, ought to give you great hope!

— D A Y   T H R E E —

Who wounded you? Have you forgiven them?

If you were the cause of your own pain, have you received God's forgiveness?

Unless you receive and give God's forgiveness, you won't be healed. If you wish to get well, you must do what Jesus says. Nothing less will suffice.

When the disciples came to Jesus in Luke 11 and asked Him to teach them how to pray, He gave them the Lord's Prayer. This prayer consisted of seven topical sentences that covered the essential ingredients of effective prayer. This same Lord's Prayer is repeated in Matthew 6:

Pray, then, in this way:
'Our Father who art in heaven,
Hallowed be Thy name.
Thy kingdom come.
Thy will be done,
On earth as it is in heaven.

Give us this day our daily bread.

And forgive us our debts, as we also have forgiven our debtors.

And do not lead us into temptation, but deliver us from evil.

[For Thine is the kingdom, and the power, and the glory, forever. Amen.]'

With that, Jesus finishes His model prayer. But He has more to say regarding forgiveness: "For if you forgive men for their transgressions, your heavenly Father will also forgive you. But if you do not forgive men, then your Father will not forgive your transgressions" (6:14-15).

1. What does this passage in Matthew 6 teach us about forgiveness? Be thorough in your answer because understanding this truth is critical to your healing.

2. One of the clearest explanations of the whole teaching on forgiveness was given by our Lord in the form of a parable. The parable was given in response to Peter's question to Jesus about how many times he had to forgive a person who transgressed against him.

Read Jesus' response very carefully. As you read, mark the word *forgive* and all of its synonyms. Ten thousand talents would have a value of about $10,000,000 in silver content, but it would be worth much more in buying power. A denarius was equivalent to one day's wage—$18.)

▶ MATTHEW 18:21-35

21 Then Peter came and said to Him, "Lord, how often shall my brother

sin against me and I forgive him? Up to seven times?

²² Jesus said to him, "I do not say to you, up to seven times, but up to seventy times seven.

²³ "For this reason the kingdom of heaven may be compared to a certain king who wished to settle accounts with his slaves.

²⁴ "And when he had begun to settle them, there was brought to him one who owed him ten thousand talents.

²⁵ "But since he did not have the means to repay, his lord commanded him to be sold, along with his wife and children and all that he had, and repayment to be made.

²⁶ "The slave therefore falling down, prostrated himself before him, saying, 'Have patience with me, and I will repay you everything.'

²⁷ "And the lord of that slave felt compassion and released him and forgave him the debt.

²⁸ "But that slave went out and found one of his fellow slaves who owed him a hundred denarii; and he seized him and began to choke him, saying, 'Pay back what you owe.'

²⁹ "So his fellow slave fell down and began to entreat him, saying, 'Have patience with me and I will repay you.'

³⁰ "He was unwilling however, but went and threw him in prison until he should pay back what was owed.

³¹ "So when his fellow slaves saw what had happened, they were deeply grieved and came and reported to their lord all that had happened.

32 "Then summoning him, his lord said to him, 'You wicked slave, I forgave you all that debt because you entreated me.

33 'Should you not also have had mercy on your fellow slave, even as I had mercy on you?'

34 "And his lord, moved with anger, handed him over to the torturers until he should repay all that was owed him.

35 "So shall My heavenly Father also do to you, if each of you does not forgive his brother from your heart."

3. Let me ask you a few questions to help clarify what our Lord is saying in this parable.
   a. What does Jesus liken these events to?

   b. Whom do you think the king represents in this parable? Why? And whom do you think the king's slave represents?

   c. What do you think Jesus is trying to show us in the situation between the two slaves—one being in debt to the other?

d. Why was the king so upset with the slave whose debt he had forgiven?

4. What was the point of the story—the bottom line? Can you see any parallels between this account and what we studied from Matthew 6? Explain your answer.

5. What have you learned from this account that you can apply to your life? Be specific.

Don't just let these things go in one ear and out the other! Think on them!

— D A Y   F O U R —

Before we talk further about forgiving others, you must realize that no matter what you have done God has assured you of complete and absolute forgiveness. It was through the blood of Jesus Christ that all your sins were paid for—once for all (Hebrews 10:10).

If you do not understand or receive the forgiveness of God, you will find it almost impossible to forgive those who have deeply hurt you or who have failed to be what they should have been to you as a mate, a mother, a father, a sister, a brother, a child, or a friend.

A guilty conscience can wreak havoc and destruction in your relationships with others, in your emotions, and even in your body. The cure for a guilty conscience comes in understanding and accepting the grace of God which freely pardons all of your sins through faith in the Lord Jesus Christ. A guilty conscience is shed like filthy rags at the foot of the throne of God in the Holy of Holies. This is why the author of Hebrews writes:

> Since therefore, brethren, we have confidence to enter the holy place by the blood of Jesus, by a new and living way which He inaugurated for us through the veil, that is, His flesh, and since we have a great priest over the house of God, let us draw near with a sincere heart in full assurance of faith, having our hearts sprinkled clean from an evil conscience and our bodies washed with pure water. (Hebrews 10:19-22)

There is no guilt that cannot be cared for at the mercy seat of God. Your part is to draw near.

There was a pastor who was as straight as an arrow doctrinally, but he hammered away unrelentingly, unlovingly at his people. His sermons were hard, his walk legalistic, and his expectations demanding. Even his wife flinched in his presence. Nothing was right. There was no pleasing him.

He used the word *love*, but it seemed to be merely head knowledge. Love's compassionate mercy was never evidenced in his life until he broke and confessed his past to a fellow believer. For years he had kept his sin bottled up inside, known only to him and a prostitute. Before going into the pastorate, he had served in the army. Based in Korea, he was given two weeks of "R&R" in Japan. There he had weakened, given in to the temporal cravings of the flesh, and visited a prostitute. He knew God's Word. He knew adultery was a sin. Yet, he had yielded.

Now, after all of his years of serving God—serving in the depth of his dedication, in the strictness of his discipline—he felt he still had not compensated for the guilt that plagued his conscience. Oh, he knew of the Cross, of Christ's death for his sins, but somehow he just couldn't accept God's forgiveness, freely bestowed, freely given for this particular, blatant sin. Because he couldn't accept God's forgiveness, it affected his relationship with his wife, and it affected his ministry as a pastor.

How far he was from portraying the Good Shepherd of the sheep, for he was a shepherd who drove his sheep rather than led them! And all because he was driven by the guilt of his sin. He sought to compensate for something that had been covered and dealt with two thousand years earlier, when Jesus cried, *"Tetelestai* —paid in full!" All he needed to do was to confess his sin and believe what God said—He would forgive him and cleanse him from all unrighteousness (1 John 1:9).

Somehow, although he understood the word *grace* to be unmerited favor, he lived under law rather than the covenant of grace. He failed to apply the truth of Hebrews 10:15-18: "And the Holy Spirit also bears witness to us; for after saying, 'THIS IS THE COVENANT THAT I WILL MAKE WITH THEM AFTER THOSE DAYS, SAYS THE LORD: I WILL PUT MY LAWS UPON THEIR HEART, AND UPON THEIR MIND I WILL WRITE THEM,' He then says, 'AND THEIR SINS AND THEIR LAWLESS DEEDS I WILL REMEMBER NO MORE.' Now where there is forgiveness of these things, there is no longer any offering for sin."

O Beloved, what will you give to pay for your sins? In your impotence, what can you do to pay back the exorbitant debt you owe our righteous and holy God? Work a lifetime? Keep all of His commandments at all times, never falter once? Always be everything you are supposed to be? Always be totally, unfailingly like Jesus. Can you do that? Of course not! Then what will you do to compensate for the times when you have been less than perfect? What will you do to compensate for the times when you have been willfully, knowingly disobedient to the will of God? Go ahead. Do your best. It won't work.

Whether your sin has been gross and blatant or delicate and disguised, there is only one way to receive God's forgiveness. It is through the blood of the Lord Jesus Christ—Jesus, the sinless One who was made sin for you, that you might be made His righteousness (2 Corinthians 5:21).

God's forgiveness is always an act of grace. It is appropriated simply by acknowledging your sin against God and receiving full pardon from Him. It is written in God's infallible word: "It is a trustworthy statement, deserving full acceptance, that Christ Jesus came into the world to save sinners" (1 Timothy 1:15).

If you refuse to believe that you are forgiven forever, you turn your back on Jesus, who paid for all of your sins, past, present, and future.

God is eager to see you walk in the reality of full forgiveness. How do you receive forgiveness? Let me give you some principles from the Scriptures that you should include as a part of your prayer.

1. First, *agree with God that what you have done is sin, a transgression against God, a rebellion against His will.* Name the sin for what it is. The English transliteration for the Greek word translated *confess* in 1 John 1:9 is *homologeō*. In the Greek, the word means "to say the same thing." To confess sin, then, is to acknowledge that what you have done is wrong in God's eyes.

2. *Take the responsibility for that sin.* You cannot blame anyone else. You made a choice to do what you did. "To one who knows the right thing to do, and does not do it, to him it is sin" (James 4:17). Acknowledge that. Take full responsibility.

3. *Tell God you are willing to make restitution to man if necessary.* Willingness to be right not only with God but also with man follows the principle laid down for us in Matthew 5:23-24: "If therefore you are presenting your offering [gift] at the altar, and there remember that your

brother has something against you, leave your offering there before the altar, and go your way; first be reconciled to your brother, and then come and present your offering."

4. *Thank God for the blood of Jesus Christ which cleanses you from all sin, and in faith accept His forgiveness.* Remember that forgiveness is always on the basis of grace, never merit. Where sin did abound, grace did much more abound (Romans 5:20).

5. *Take God at His Word:* "There is therefore now no condemnation for those who are in Christ Jesus" (Romans 8:1). No matter the feelings, in faith cling to what God says. Don't allow the accuser, Satan, to rob you of faith's victory.

6. *Thank God for the gift of His Holy Spirit and tell Him that you want to walk by the Spirit so that you will not fulfill the lusts of the flesh* (Galatians 5:16).

Go before God now and, remembering these principles, ask Him for forgiveness. A prayer based on these will show a genuine desire for repentance.

— D A Y   F I V E —

Having received forgiveness, how are you to respond toward those who have sinned against you? Possibly your mate, your parent(s), your child, your friend, or your neighbor has not fulfilled the debt owed you by virtue of a proper relationship. Do you need to forgive them because they weren't what they should have been to you?

Maybe your wife constantly put you down or withheld herself from you sexually. Maybe your husband abused or neglected you instead of loving you as God commands. Maybe your parents neglected you, demeaned you, abused you, failed in their responsibility to care for you. Maybe your neighbors or friends took advantage of you instead of loving you as they would love themselves. Maybe someone hurt or wounded your loved one.

How are you to respond to them? In order to answer that question, we need to see what God has to say in His Word. Look up the following scriptures, and record what you learn from them regarding the how, whys, and wherefores of forgiveness.

1. Ephesians 4:31-32 (Do you see the connection that bitterness, anger, wrath, clamor, and slander have with unforgiveness? Explain your insights as you look at these verses.)

2. Colossians 3:12-15 (As you look at these verses, do you see any correlation between the character and lifestyle that God is calling us to and the admonition to forgive others?)

3. Finally, how does what you have seen in Colossians and Ephesians relate to what you saw two days ago in your study of Matthew 18:21-35 and Matthew 6:8,12,14-15?

The greatest expression of God's love was seen at Calvary's cross when Jesus said, "Father, forgive them; for they do not know what they are doing" (Luke 23:34). Love forgives.

Think about it, and then tomorrow we'll talk about why it is sometimes so hard to forgive.

– D A Y   S I X –

When we have suffered unjustly at the hands of others, it is hard to forgive, especially if they won't admit it or aren't sorry for what they did. Many times we have no desire to forgive. How can we, when they have been so awful, so unjust? When they have hurt us or the ones we love?

What do you do when you feel that you can't forgive or there is no desire to do so?

1. *You must realize that forgiveness is a matter of the will, not the emotions. To forgive or not to forgive is a matter of choice.* Since God has commanded us to forgive others, not to do so is to refuse to obey God. Commands are not options or suggestions that we can pick or choose from on the basis of our emotions or desires. Rather, commands are orders issued by our Lord which are to be obeyed, regardless of what we feel or think. Let this sink in.

2. *You need to realize that your forgiveness of another does not let that person off the hook with God.* Your forgiveness of others doesn't exempt them from the just judgment of God. It doesn't mean that they won't be held accountable for what they have done.

Let's look at this statement very carefully and point by point.

a. All sin will be judged by God, along with the deeds or works which accompany all of our actions. If a person does not believe on the Lord Jesus Christ so as to be saved, then "there no longer remains a sacrifice for sins, but a certain terrifying expectation of judgment, and THE FURY OF A FIRE WHICH WILL CONSUME THE ADVERSARIES" (Hebrews 10:26-27).

"For after all it is only just for God to repay with affliction those who afflict you, and to give relief to you who are afflicted and to us as well when the Lord Jesus shall be revealed from heaven with His mighty angels in flaming fire, dealing out retribution to those who do not know God and to those who do not obey the gospel of our Lord Jesus. And these will pay the penalty of eternal destruction, away from the presence of the Lord and from the glory of His power" (2 Thessalonians 1:6-9).

b. Jesus bore mankind's sins in His body, yet He forgave those who transgressed against Him when He hung on the cross. However, if they do not repent and believe on Him, they will still go to hell. Forgiveness is offered, but it is not apart from receiving Jesus Christ. I know that many of you have borne others' sins in your body also, as they have physically, emotionally, sexually, and mentally abused you. Yet, my precious one, you are to forgive them, just as Christ forgave those who transgressed against Him.

c. You are to manifest the character and love of Jesus Christ by forgiving as He forgave you. If you refuse to forgive, you keep people from seeing the character of Christ. You are the only Bible many people will ever read. Therefore, you are to be a living epistle known and read by all men. When you forgive, you are demonstrating the character of God. You are modeling the love of God by forgiving "even as Jesus forgave you."

d. When your forgiveness does not lead others to repentance, then they will be held even more accountable to God. They are left without excuse. They have seen with their own eyes and heard with their own ears a demonstration of the reality of the gospel of Jesus Christ. How clearly this principle of "greater accountability" is brought out in scriptures such as Matthew 11:21-24; 12:41-42; and Revelation 20:11-13.

3. If you are having a hard time, if you are wrestling with forgiving another, *you need to ask God to let you take a good, hard, objective look at the Lord's forgiveness of you.* Remember that when you forgive someone, it is one sinner forgiving another. Neither you nor the other person is or has been what you ought to be. However, it is different in the case of man receiving forgiveness from God. When Jesus Christ forgives us, He is forgiving someone who has sinned against His perfect holiness!

Take a few minutes to read Luke 7:36-50, and then answer the questions that follow.

▶ LUKE 7:36-50

36 Now one of the Pharisees was requesting Him to dine with him. And He entered the Pharisee's house, and reclined at the table.

37 And behold, there was a woman in the city who was a sinner; and when she learned that He was reclining at the table in the Pharisee's house, she brought an alabaster vial of perfume,

38 and standing behind Him at His feet, weeping, she began to wet His feet with her tears, and kept wiping them with the hair of her head, and kissing His feet, and anointing them with the perfume.

39 Now when the Pharisee who had invited Him saw this, he said to himself, "If this man were a prophet He would know who and what sort of person this woman is who is touching Him, that she is a sinner."

40 And Jesus answered and said to him, "Simon, I have something to say to you." And he replied, "Say it, Teacher."

41 "A certain moneylender had two debtors: one owed five hundred denarii, and the other fifty.

42 "When they were unable to repay, he graciously forgave them both. Which of them therefore will love him more?"

43 Simon answered and said, "I suppose the one whom he forgave more." And He said to him, "You have judged correctly."

44 And turning toward the woman, He said to Simon, "Do you see this woman? I entered your house; you gave Me no water for My feet, but she has wet My feet with her tears, and wiped them with her hair.

45 "You gave Me no kiss; but she, since the time I came in, has not ceased to kiss My feet.

46 "You did not anoint My head with oil, but she anointed My feet with perfume.

47 "For this reason I say to you, her sins, which are many, have been forgiven, for she loved much; but he who is forgiven little, loves little."

48 And He said to her, "Your sins have been forgiven."

49 And those who were reclining at the table with Him began to say to themselves, "Who is this man who even forgives sins?"

50 And He said to the woman, "Your faith has saved you; go in peace."

1. How would you describe the Pharisee in this historical account?

2. What do you learn about the woman in this account?

3. What was the point of the story Jesus told to Simon the Pharisee?

4. Contrast the love of the Pharisee and the love of the woman. Weren't they both sinners? What made the difference in their responses to our Lord?

— D A Y   S E V E N —

The more you comprehend the greatness of God's forgiveness of you, the more you will love. The more you love, the easier it is to forgive "just as God in Christ also has forgiven you. Therefore be imitators of God, as beloved children; and walk in love, just as Christ also loved you, and gave Himself up for us, an offering and a sacrifice to God as a fragrant aroma" (Ephesians 4:32–5:2).

Let me share once again what Karen wrote regarding her healing from her uncle's incestuous abuse.

The issue of forgiveness had to be confronted. I visited a dear and trusted friend, also a victim of incest. I had witnessed her peace, contentment and radiant joy in Christ, and I needed to know how she had attained that victory. She related that it had been in a moment of crisis when her marriage was about to fall apart that she knelt and thanked God for giving her the parents He had wanted her to have. And then she expressed gratitude for each person and circumstance of life that God had allowed to touch hers. As she praised and thanked God, she expressed her forgiveness for what her father had done to her, and she got up from her knees and began to walk in forgiveness and acceptance. God salvaged her marriage.

I came home and, in the presence of my pastor, prayed and released my uncle (now deceased) and all others who had offended me from any debt I had felt they owed me. Then I spent another period of prayer alone going through my past, thanking God for being with me through it all, for knowing my downsitting and my uprising, and for being intimately acquainted with all my ways, as Psalms 139:1-6 says. During this prayer God reminded me of many things which He had said of me, His child, in His Word, which I had been rejecting. I recorded each verse as He brought these truths to mind. It was exciting to have God communicating with me in prayer.

Karen forgave, and the result was a deep intimacy in her relationship with God because they were one in heart in forgiveness.

Beloved, will you walk in obedience and forgive, even as Christ Jesus forgave you? To refuse to forgive is to sin. To obey and forgive is to say, "God, I love You, and I am willing to sacrifice self and its desires." To that, Jesus says, "If anyone loves Me, he will keep My word; and My Father will love him, and We will come to him, and make Our abode with him" (John 14:23). What fellowship, what intimacy obedience brings!

I urge you to take a few moments right now and review what you have learned about forgiveness. Remember that forgiveness is a matter of your will, a choice to obey God regardless of your emotions. Use these next few moments to ask the Lord to forgive you for your unforgiveness toward those who have wronged you. Will you cry out to your loving heavenly Father and tell Him that you choose to forgive those persons who have hurt you or who have hurt those whom you love? You might want to write out your prayer to Him.

True forgiveness of another will also bring love. Hatred for that person will be replaced by love. As I speak of love, I am not speaking of a sentiment. I am speaking of an action. As you see when you read through the Bible, *love* is an action verb. Therefore, if you say you have forgiven a person, and you don't want to have anything to do with him, you need to go back to God and ask Him what is keeping you from loving the person.

Forgiveness and love are like Siamese twins which cannot be separated. Stop and think of love's associations. Love is part of the ninefold fruit of the Spirit—love, joy, peace.... As "imitators of God," you are to "walk in love, just as Christ also loved you, and gave Himself up for us, an offering and a sacrifice to God as a fragrant aroma" (Ephesians 5:1-2).

You may have a difficult time loving someone you have forgiven, but true forgiveness will make the sacrifice. Jesus didn't forgive you and then refuse to love you. He forgives and treats you as if you never sinned against Him. That's God's forgiveness. And your forgiveness is to be like God's. "If someone says, 'I love God,' and hates his brother, he is a liar; for the one who does not love his brother whom he has seen, cannot love God whom he has not seen. And this commandment we have from Him, that the one who loves God should love his brother also" (1 John 4:20-21).

If you are saying that you cannot love, you may have to deal with anger and bitterness in order to really forgive. We will look at that in the final two weeks. But today won't you say, "God, out of sheer obedience, I want to forgive. Help me." If you will, record it by writing it out.

MEMORY VERSE

"For I know the plans that I have for you," declares the LORD, "plans for welfare and not for calamity to give you a future and a hope."

JEREMIAH 29:11

SMALL-GROUP DISCUSSION QUESTIONS

In week ten you learned that your enemy, Satan, has an army, a demonic host. You saw that you are truly in a warfare, and you saw some of the enemy's tactics. But you also learned what your weapons are and how to use them.

You learned how to respond to the affliction in your life, and you saw that those situations can also be used to minister to others.

1. Is it possible for everyone to be healed from the wounds of the past, from the hurts, the disappointments, the tragedies? What does the healing depend upon?
2. What is the basic reason that people are not made whole? Why had the man at the pool not been healed?
3. Why do some people choose not to be healed?
4. In order to be healed, you must be willing to forgive others, or you must be willing to accept God's forgiveness for yourself. What did you learn about forgiveness in this lesson?
5. What did you learn from Joseph's life?
   a. What were the circumstances of his situation?

    b. What did he suffer as a result?

    c. What was his response in all of this?

    d. Was there unforgiveness or bitterness in his life?

6. What did you learn in Luke 7 about how sin should be viewed?

7. What did you learn about forgiveness in Luke 7?

    a. What is the result of forgiveness?

    b. How often are you to forgive?

8. What was the point of the parable that Jesus told in Matthew 18?

    a. Whom does the king represent? Why?

    b. Whom does the king's slave represent?

    c. Why was the king so upset with the slave whose debt he had for-given?

    d. What parallels can you draw from this story?

9. What did you learn from the other passages you studied this week on forgiveness? How are you to respond to those who have hurt you?

10. Why wouldn't a person want to forgive?

11. What do you do when you have no desire to forgive? What will happen if you refuse to forgive?

12. What will the result of true forgiveness be?

13. How do you plan to respond to the great truths of this lesson? If you respond properly (biblically), what will the result be?

BUT I'M SO ANGRY!

— D A Y   O N E —

I had just finished teaching on forgiveness at our Singles Conference when she came barreling down the center aisle. Dressed in a sloppy gray sweatshirt and jeans which stretched across a little roll of fat that dropped down below her waist like a small inner tube, this woman was not one who enjoyed her femininity. Her dark hair hung from her head in greasy strands in stark contrast to the whiteness of her face that didn't have one bit of makeup on it.

I had never seen nor met the woman before, and yet her first words were "I can't forgive my father." Blurted out through taut lips, it was obvious I was talking to a woman who was suffering greatly. Why? I didn't know. But I intended to find out.

I took her gently by the arm, ushered her to the edge of the platform away from the people, and seated her so that her back would be to the auditorium.

"Now, darlin', tell me why you can't forgive your father. What has he done to you?" I asked, praying that God would give me great wisdom and that He would love this woman through me.

"My father got me pregnant and then made me have an abortion. Then he got me pregnant again, and this time I had the baby. But my baby was deformed and died. He said that I was a slut, that I had been messing around with boys. But that was a lie. After all that my dad did to me, I didn't want anyone to touch me. Then he got me pregnant again, and this time I moved out. My baby was born deformed, but she lived for a year. When she died, I didn't want to live. I tried to kill myself. They put me in a mental hospital and said that I had to have group therapy with my family. When I told them what my father did to me, he jumped up, pointed his finger at me, and yelled that I was lying and that I was a no-good slut, just a tramp. My mother jumped up and yelled the same thing at me. So I shut my mouth, and I didn't say a word for months. I cannot forgive my father."

As suddenly as she began her story, talking almost without breathing, she stopped. She hadn't looked at me the whole time. She had stared only at her feet.

My immediate response to this horrible account was "That makes me so angry."

With that, her head shot up as she said, "What?"

"What your father did to you. It makes me angry."

Her big brown eyes searched mine. Tears began rolling down her cheeks. "No one has ever said that before," she said, as I reached up to wipe the tears off her chin. Her words were so soft, so incredibly tender.

"Oh, darlin', not only does it make me angry, but it makes God angry too. Far more angry. God hates what your father did to you."

These were our first words to each other—words that initiated her healing process. A healing that began when she discovered that God also was angry at her father's sin. That weekend she chose to forgive her father.

Three years passed, and in that time God did miraculous things in this woman! I won't take time to tell you all of the wonderful things that happened, but I want you to know that now she loves being a woman. You wouldn't recognize her as the same person. She has lost weight, takes good care of herself, is married, and recently became a mother. No longer is she afraid of her femininity. No longer does she hide it for fear it might be violated. She has learned to lean upon God's Word, to trust Him as a Father she never knew.

How wonderful it was to watch God heal her. I think her healing happened so quickly because she became putty in His sovereign hands of love. It all began when my friend was willing to give her anger and bitterness to God and to forgive her father.

Would you be willing to do the same, or are you too consumed by anger to let your anger and bitterness go so that you might be willing and able to forgive? Write out your answer to this question. This is a question you need to face quite squarely if you want to be healed.

This week I want us to concentrate on anger. I want us to understand this emotion, which is not always wrong, but which, if not handled properly, can wreak havoc in you and in your relationship with God and with others.

— D A Y   T W O —

Contrary to some people's opinions, anger is not always a sin. As I expressed in the incident of my friend and her father, there is a righteous anger. God gets angry. His anger is totally justified and is provoked only by sin. One cannot read the Old Testament or Revelation without seeing the anger of God or the consequences of His wrath. Sin—disobedience— does not leave God passive. His righteousness demands indignation, anger, and wrath at that which goes against His character, at that which violates His commandments and precepts. As a matter of fact, you will recall that we studied God's wrath when we looked at His attributes.

If you and I are going to learn to deal with our anger in a biblical way so that we might be healed, it will help to understand God's anger.

The words *anger, angered,* and *angry* are used approximately 364 times in the Old and New Testaments.[1] Most of these references are to God's anger. Therefore, let me share with you some of the things that make God angry.

As I list these, I will give you scripture references to look up and write out.

God is angered...

1. *by injustice:* Exodus 22:22-24

2. *by idolatry:* Deuteronomy 29:18-21; Jeremiah 25:6

3. *by spiritual adultery*—when we mingle with the world, learn its practices, serve its idols, and sacrifice our children to "demons" through our disobedience: Psalm 106:34-40

4. *when He is betrayed:* Deuteronomy 4:23-26

5. *when He is not listened to:* Jeremiah 25:6-11 (Remember all that you have learned from Jeremiah about listening to God!)

6. *by disobedience to Him:* Joshua 7:1

7. *when His people complain and murmur against Him or His servants:* Numbers 11:1,33; 12:1-9

8. *by unbelief:* Psalm 78:21-22; Hebrews 3:7-12; John 3:36 (Notice the word *wrath* is used here, which points more to the end result of His righteous anger.)

9. *by the ungodliness and unrighteousness of men who suppress truth in unrighteousness:* Romans 1:18 (Note again the use of the word *wrath.*)

10. *when we refuse to pay homage to His Son:* Psalm 2:10-12

Now that you have seen what angers God, there are several other things I want you to see in regard to God's anger.

First of all, God's anger is His response to sin, to unbelief (all unbelief is sin). When we read of God's anger, we need to remember that, although His anger is provoked by man's sin, He is never controlled by His anger. God's anger is always kept in balance by His holiness—and by all of those attributes which make Him God.

Therefore, when God expresses anger, it is always within the realm of His character—never contrary to it. His anger is always in harmony with His grace, His love, His mercy, His compassion, and His long-suffering. It is always expressed with the intent of ultimate good and justice and not of evil. "For His anger is but for a moment, His favor is for a lifetime; weeping may last for the night, but a shout of joy comes in the morning" (Psalm 30:5).

This truth is seen throughout the Word of God. How well it is explained in Exodus 34:6-7: "The LORD, the LORD God, compassionate and gracious, slow to anger, and abounding in lovingkindness and truth; who keeps lovingkindness for thousands, who forgives iniquity, transgression and sin; yet He will by no means leave the guilty unpunished."

You might want to look at the entire passage from Exodus 33 and 34 where God deals with Israel's idolatry at the time of the giving of the Ten Commandments.

Second, God is slow to anger. This statement is made of Him about nine times in the Old Testament. "But Thou, O Lord, art a God merciful and gracious, slow to anger and abundant in lovingkindness and truth" (Psalm 86:15).

Third, our Lord Jesus, God in the flesh, felt anger. Remember the two different times—once at the beginning of His public ministry and the other at the end—when He turned over the tables of the moneychangers in the temple? He was righteously angry, and yet He was righteously controlled as He drove them out with a whip. We know from the testimony of Scripture that Jesus always handled His anger in a way pleasing to His Father because He always and only did those things which pleased the Father (John 8:28-29).

What a lesson is here for us! Justified or not, *anger is never to control us.* We are to be controlled by the Spirit of God. Therefore, our response must be according to His total character. The moment we are manifesting anything but His heart, we are in trouble.

We have looked at anger for three reasons. First I want you to see that all anger is not bad, that there is an anger which is justified. Second, I want you to see that anger is never to control you, even if it is justified. When anger takes control of you, then you are in trouble because the wrath of man does not work the righteousness of God (James 1:19-20). Finally, I want you to see that anger is an emotion experienced by God as well as by man. Consequently, you and I can know that God understands the emotion of anger and how it can inflame and burn within. However, *we must never forget that God's anger is always justified!* Our anger may or may not be justified.

Tomorrow we will begin looking at the anger of man—anger as expressed not only toward man, but also toward God. Then in the days to come, we will look at what happens when anger is not dealt with in a biblical way. However, we will not stop there. We will also see how to deal with our anger biblically so that healing can come into our lives.

— D A Y   T H R E E —

Today, we are going to look at man's anger toward God. You can't harbor anger in your heart toward God and be healed, Beloved. So we need to see what causes people to become angry with God and why anger is never justifiable.

Why do people get angry at God?

1. *Anger can come because God doesn't operate or conform to our ways or to our understanding.* How well this is seen in Genesis 4:1-8. Cain wanted to worship God his way, and he became angry when God rejected his sacrifice.

Those who have been hurt by people or circumstances get angry because they do not understand why, if God is a God of love, He would allow such things to happen to them or to someone they love. This type of anger was demonstrated by the hurting woman who said to me out of great bitterness, "When God gives me back my baby, then I'll believe in Him." Her precious baby had died in a fire.

2. *Anger can come because of God's judgment.* In 1 Chronicles 13:11, David gets mad at God because He kills Uzzah for touching the ark of the covenant. In Revelation, men get mad at God for His judgments upon the earth. Even today, there are many who are suffering because of the consequences of their own sin. Yet they are angry with God because He judged them.

3. *Anger can come because we don't like the words of God's servants.*
Although this type of anger is seen in so many scriptures, for time's sake
let me give you just two. King Asa gets mad at Hanani when he rebukes
him for not relying on the Lord. In his anger, Asa puts Hanani in prison
(2 Chronicles 16:7-10). The same thing happened to Jeremiah for deliver-
ing God's Word.

There are people who will not be healed because they don't like what
God says. It makes them angry when you tell them they must put away
their bitterness, forgive their transgressors, God is sovereign.... They walk
away with a parting sentence something like this: "Well, if that's the God
of the Bible, then you can just forget it. I don't want anything to do with
that kind of a God!" They are cutting themselves off from Jehovah-rapha
and His healing balm. How tragic!

4. *Anger can come because God doesn't judge others when we want Him
to.* Jonah got mad at God and pouted under the shade of a gourd because
God wouldn't destroy the Ninevites, whom he hated (Jonah 4:1-11). As I
write this, I think of those who are angry and bitter toward God for allowing the Holocaust and for not destroying Hitler before he committed all
of those horrible atrocities. We will cover this type of anger later when we
look at Psalm 37.

Beloved, you need to ask the Holy Spirit to search your heart to see if
you have any unresolved anger which you have harbored against God.
Get alone in a quiet place, and give yourself uninterrupted time with
Him. If the phone rings, just don't answer it. Turn off the radio, the television, the stereo, and be still. Find a piece of paper and a pen, and write
down what God brings to your mind. Then I will share with you what
you need to do with what God shows you. If He does not show you anything, then pray for others who are doing this study. Intercede for their
total healing.

Finally, let's look at how one deals with anger toward God. Read Isaiah 45:20-24, and then I will give you some insights to ponder.

▶ ISAIAH 45:20-24

20 Gather yourselves and come; draw near together, you fugitives of the nations; they have no knowledge, who carry about their wooden idol, and pray to a god who cannot save.

21 Declare and set forth your case; indeed, let them consult together. Who has announced this from of old? Who has long since declared it? Is it not I, the LORD? And there is no other God besides Me, a righteous God and a Savior; there is none except Me.

22 Turn to Me, and be saved, all the ends of the earth; for I am God, and there is no other.

23 I have sworn by Myself, the word has gone forth from My mouth in righteousness and will not turn back, that to Me every knee will bow, every tongue will swear allegiance.

24 They will say of Me, "Only in the LORD are righteousness and strength." Men will come to Him, and all who were angry at Him shall be put to shame.

If you are angry at God, I would suggest that you:

1. *"Declare and set forth your case."* Use what you wrote out a few minutes ago and talk out your anger with God. Verbalize it. Tell God why you are angry. You might want to write it out below.

2. *Turn to God.* Tell Him you recognize that He is God and that because He is, He does not have to answer to you. He can do whatever He pleases.

3. *Be put to shame for your prideful rebellion in being angry with Him. Confess your sin.* If you have been angry at God, you have set yourself as His judge. You have said in your heart that God is wrong in His dealings and that He is wrong in His character. You, mere man, in your anger have thought you knew better than God! You determined what was good and what was evil, rather than allowing God to judge it. That is pride. Let it be put to shame. Confess that righteousness is only in Him, that in and of yourself there is no righteousness.

4. *Humble yourself before God. Bow the knee. Submit to Him.*

5. *With your mouth, your tongue, swear allegiance to Him as your God, your Lord, your Master.* And "in the LORD," you "will be justified, and will glory" (Isaiah 45:25). Hallelujah and Amen!

— D A Y   F O U R —

Just the other day I got so angry at my husband that I could hardly stand it. Now this response is not the norm for me. Jack and I get along wonderfully, and I am so thankful for that! However, this was an exception on my part.

I was getting ready to go out when something came up that made me unhappy. Thinking Jack would want to know about it, I began to share with him. As I was telling him a disappointment, he changed the subject right in the middle of our conversation. He asked me if I had recorded a check in the checkbook. He had seen the checkbook lying on my desk while we were standing there talking, so he asked! Now if you are a man, there may seem to be nothing wrong with such an action, but if you are a woman, I am sure you can understand how I felt.

Anger took over! And I sinned. Instead of dealing with my anger, I ran it full speed. I blew it! I was headed for the grocery store, so I left immediately. Jerking up my keys from my desk, I trounced out of our bedroom, slammed a book on the bench in our entrance hall, and charged out the front door. Now I have to tell you that I haven't done something like this in years—not since just before I wrote our "Marriage Without Regrets" course!

The whole time I knew I was wrong. Anger was controlling me. I was walking in the flesh. And although I didn't think Jack should have picked up the checkbook or should have changed the subject, unfortunately that did not excuse my behavior. I had to come back and ask forgiveness.

Why did I get angry? We always need to stop and ask ourselves this question when we feel the emotion rising within us. It helps us evaluate the situation and then handle it in a way that is pleasing to God. Therefore, I want us to look at some incidents from the Word of God where others found themselves in situations where they became angry.

Why do people get angry?

1. *Anger can come when people do not deal fairly with us.* This was the case of David and Nabal. David protected Nabal's flocks, but Nabal would not return the favor by giving David's men a share of his harvest. This infuriated David, who went out to destroy Nabal. It was Nabal's wife, Abigail, who brought David to his senses when she asked him to forgive her husband: "Let no wrongdoing be found in you as long as you live" (1 Samuel 25:28, NIV). David forgave Nabal. David brought his anger under God's control. God dealt with Nabal.

2. *Anger can come when we see others are not treated properly.* Jonathan's feelings toward his father, King Saul, portray this well. Jonathan was angry over Saul's treatment of David. "Then Jonathan arose from the table in

fierce anger, and did not eat food on the second day of the new moon, for he was grieved over David because his father had dishonored him" (1 Samuel 20:34).

Doesn't this kind of anger and hurt come when one lives with an alcoholic who abuses the family? When children suffer through a divorce in the family? When one lives with an angry or abusive person? The anger comes, but it must be dealt with, for *to harbor anger is sin*. Unchecked, anger can cause you to mistreat others.

3. *Anger can come just from seeing or knowing the sins of others.* Moses certainly experienced this type of anger several times in his leadership of the children of Israel. Look at Exodus 32:19. But in Numbers 20:2-13, Moses allowed his anger to rule him. He struck the rock a second time, although God told him to speak to the rock. That outburst of anger cost Moses the promised land. After forty years of wandering in the wilderness, he never entered the land of Canaan because he had responded to the Israelites in anger instead of obeying God. God said to him, "Because you have not believed Me, to treat Me as holy in the sight of the sons of Israel, therefore you shall not bring this assembly into the land which I have given them" (Numbers 20:12).

4. *Anger can come from fear of losing our position or our standing with others.* Jealousy can cause anger. This type of anger is so evident in Saul's response to the praise given David. As the women sang, "Saul has slain his thousands, and David his ten thousands," Saul became very angry, "for this saying displeased him; and he said, 'They have ascribed to David ten thousands, but to me they have ascribed thousands. Now what more can he have but the kingdom?'" (1 Samuel 18:7-8). After this incident Saul wanted to kill David.

Remember when Tom slapped me? That whole scene was provoked because Tom was angry that I had found satisfaction and success in modeling, while he was so unhappy in his job. Do you see how crucial it is that you deal with your anger, "for the anger of man does not achieve the righteousness of God" (James 1:20)?

5. *Anger can come simply because we feel under pressure, inconvenienced, or interrupted. Or anger may result just because we are irritated by another's personality or behavior.* This anger is seen in 1 Samuel 17:28-29 when David visits his brothers while their army is being challenged by Goliath. Watch carefully Eliab's words and David's use of the word *now.* "Now Eliab his oldest brother heard when he [David] spoke to the men; and Eliab's anger burned against David and he said, 'Why have you come down? And with whom have you left those few sheep in the wilderness? I know your insolence and the wickedness of your heart; for you have come down in order to see the battle.' But David said, 'What have I done now? Was it not just a question?' "

6. *Anger can come toward those whose expectations we cannot fulfill.* For example, when Rachel gets upset with Jacob because he does not give her children, he becomes angry: "Then Jacob's anger burned against Rachel, and he said, 'Am I in the place of God, who has withheld from you the fruit of the womb?' " (Genesis 30:2).

Many children, mates, and even parents are hurt and angry because they could not fill their loved ones' expectations. Many who are effeminate, homosexuals, and lesbians couldn't be the man or the woman their parent(s) wanted, and in their anger and frustration, they turned to the same sex for love and acceptance, instead of turning to God.

7. *Anger can come from having our sins exposed by others.* Sinners do not like to be found out. Their fury can be great. We have already seen this in Jeremiah's life. We also see that men stoned the prophets God sent them. Guess why Balaam beat his donkey (Numbers 22:21-35)?

8. *Anger can come from personal pride.* When our pride is hurt, we are tempted to become angry. Pride is of the flesh. Cross the flesh, and it is going to get indignant. When King Amaziah sent home a group of soldiers before they were allowed to ever fight in a battle, the soldiers became angry. "Then Amaziah dismissed them, the troops which came to him from Ephraim, to go home; so their anger burned against Judah and they returned home in fierce anger" (2 Chronicles 25:10).

Our three sons played soccer, so I've been to a lot of soccer games. Sometimes when a player missed a crucial kick, pass, or goal, he would pound his fist on the ground, get angry, and stomp all over the place. What happened? He was mad at himself. His pride was injured. We taught our sons that they were never to display their anger in this way. They were to give their mistakes and failures to the Lord and get on with the game. If you are still seething over the past inadequacies of your flesh, give that to the Lord and get back in the game.

9. *Anger can come from being embarrassed by others.* King Ahasuerus experienced this type of anger when Vashti would not do as he asked. "After these things when the anger of King Ahasuerus had subsided, he remembered Vashti and what she had done and what had been decreed against her" (Esther 2:1). Sometimes women or men who turn against their mates, divorce them, or seek to hurt them physically are reacting to pent-up anger which has come because they have been humiliated and/or embarrassed for years by their mates.

10. *Anger can also come against those who condemn others or against those who justify themselves before God or before others.* Elihu's anger against Job and against his three "friends" illustrates this type of anger (Job 32:1-4).

11. *Anger can come because of the sins of others.* Absalom burned with anger until he killed his brother Amnon because Amnon had forced himself on his sister Tamar, robbing her of her virginity (2 Samuel 13). Tamar was David's daughter, and when Amnon violated her, although David was angry, he did not allow his anger to control him. However, Absalom was a man who never dealt with his anger, even toward his father, and eventually it resulted in his death.

How vital it is that we give this anger to God! Remember only God has the right to avenge sin. He alone is just and holy. He will avenge according to His character. Now as I say this, I also want to say that if God tells us how to deal with particular sins, then we are to carry out His judgments as He tells us in His Word.

12. *Anger can come when the wickedness of man continues seemingly*

unchecked. We'll look at this in detail tomorrow as we study Psalm 37. So hangeth thou in there!

— D A Y   F I V E —

Have you ever been angry at the wicked and their deeds? I have. If it were not for what I know of God's Word, their seemingly unhindered wickedness would give me an ulcer.

What can you learn from God's Word that will help you keep your anger in check? Let's look at the first portion of Psalm 37. There are practical truths in this psalm that will help you greatly.

Read through Psalm 37:1-15, and mark the following words in a distinctive way so that you can spot them immediately:

a. fret

b. anger

c. every reference to God or the Lord, along with their pronouns

d. evildoers, wrongdoers, wicked (Mark all of these the same way.)

e. trust

f. wait, rest

▶ PSALM 37:1-15

1 Do not fret because of evildoers, be not envious toward wrongdoers.

2 For they will wither quickly like the grass, and fade like the green herb.

3 Trust in the LORD, and do good; dwell in the land and cultivate faithfulness.

4 Delight yourself in the LORD; and He will give you the desires of your heart.

5 Commit your way to the LORD, trust also in Him, and He will do it.

6 And He will bring forth your righteousness as the light, and your judgment as the noonday.

7 Rest in the LORD and wait patiently for Him; do not fret because of him who prospers in his way, because of the man who carries out wicked schemes.

8 Cease from anger, and forsake wrath; do not fret, it leads only to evildoing.

9 For evildoers will be cut off, but those who wait for the LORD, they will inherit the land.

10 Yet a little while and the wicked man will be no more; and you will look carefully for his place, and he will not be there.

11 But the humble will inherit the land, and will delight themselves in abundant prosperity.

12 The wicked plots against the righteous, and gnashes at him with his teeth.

13 The Lord laughs at him; for He sees his day is coming.

14 The wicked have drawn the sword and bent their bow, to cast down the afflicted and the needy, to slay those who are upright in conduct.

15 Their sword will enter their own heart, and their bows will be broken.

1. List below what you've learned from marking the words in Psalm 37.

2. What are God's exhortations or commands to you in Psalm 37:1-15? List these.

    While this psalm is fresh on your mind, there are some principles I want you to focus on.

    In Psalm 37 we see that we are not to fret over evildoers. The way to deal with anger is to refrain from it, to turn away from it. Fretting leads to anger and to sin. In the midst of frustration and anger over evildoers, you and I are to delight ourselves in our Lord.

    When God tells us to delight ourselves in Him, He is turning our attention to our one and only source of satisfaction—Him. Our hurts have come or been compounded when we have placed our expectations of happiness and fulfillment in others rather than in God. Or when we looked to the attainment of things for our happiness rather than to the Lord Himself. He is the One who gives us the desires of our heart, not man.

    O Beloved, have you ever thought that maybe the reason you have hurt so badly is because you sought from man what only God could give? Maybe that is why you are so angry at your loved one. Your delight has been in the arm of flesh rather than in the Lord Himself...and the flesh will always fail. God won't.

The second way you can deal with anger, according to Psalm 37, is to realize that it is God who shapes your future, not man. Peace, rather than frustration and anger, will come as you commit your way unto Him, trust in Him, and wait patiently until He brings it to pass. The will of your Sovereign God will not be thwarted. Therefore, don't allow man to frustrate you or cause you to do evil. Trust in your God, the One who causes all things to work together for your good. Trust is a great cure for anger.

Finally, Psalm 37 assures us that we do not need to vent our anger on evildoers. God will deal with them because He sees the day of the wicked coming when "their sword will enter their own heart, and their bows will be broken" (37:13,15). He reminds us to follow our Lord's example who "while being reviled, He did not revile in return; while suffering, He uttered no threats, but kept entrusting Himself to Him (God the Father) who judges righteously" (1 Peter 2:23).

– D A Y   S I X –

Anger can be very destructive and dangerous. Newspapers and the evening news confirm this fact daily as they give reports of killings, murders, riots, and international conflicts. Anger can lead to strife, dissension, conflict, and murder.

Anger may not be detected until it explodes. Often we read of people going on a rampage and killing numerous people for no apparent reason—like the man who walked into a McDonald's restaurant and gunned down innocent people, or the student who went on a shooting spree in his high school, or the placid postal clerk who went on a destructive rampage. What is going on? If you could know the background of each incident, you would find that each was harboring unresolved anger and bitterness.

How crucial it is that we learn to deal with anger immediately!

How can one know if anger has not been dealt with? If it's being held within and stored up? What happens when anger is not dealt with and released to God? Let me give you a list of insights I have gleaned from the Word. Look up the scriptures and note what you learn.

1. Anger seeks revenge: Genesis 49:6-7; 1 Samuel 25:28,31

2. Anger is laid up (is collected in the heart): Job 36:13

and smolders and burns: Hosea 7:6; Proverbs 30:33

and then...

3. Anger stirs up strife: Proverbs 29:22

4. Anger becomes a flood (i.e., suddenly gushing out, overwhelming, covering): Proverbs 27:4

5. Anger bears grudges: Psalm 55:3

6. Anger accuses: 1 Samuel 17:28

7. Anger brings sinful actions (transgressions): Proverbs 29:22

8. Anger can cut us off from friends: Proverbs 22:24-25

9. Anger causes us to despise people (Many times this is manifested in the way that we talk to them or about them. Murder begins in the heart.): Matthew 5:22

Unreleased anger will eventually lead to bitterness. Bitterness unchecked causes trouble and defiles many (Hebrews 12:15). If you are to be healed, you must deal with anger and bitterness before they destroy you and those around you.

— D A Y   S E V E N —

How do you handle anger?

We have finally come to the time when we need to see how to deal with anger toward man.

Let's begin with a look at Ephesians 4:26.

1. Write out Ephesians 4:26 and memorize it.

2. List the two things you learn from Ephesians 4:26 about responding
to anger.

Ephesians 4:26 begins with a quote from Psalm 4:4: "Be angry, and
yet do not sin." Read Psalm 4 and answer the questions which follow.

 PSALM 4

¹ Answer me when I call, O God of my righteousness! Thou hast relieved
me in my distress; be gracious to me and hear my prayer.

² O sons of men, how long will my honor become a reproach? How long
will you love what is worthless and aim at deception?

³ But know that the LORD has set apart the godly man for Himself; the
LORD hears when I call to Him.

⁴ Tremble, and do not sin; meditate in your heart upon your bed, and be
still.

⁵ Offer the sacrifices of righteousness, and trust in the LORD.

⁶ Many are saying, "Who will show us any good?" Lift up the light of
Thy countenance upon us, O LORD!

⁷ Thou hast put gladness in my heart, more than when their grain and
new wine abound.

⁸ In peace I will both lie down and sleep, for Thou alone, O LORD, dost
make me to dwell in safety.

As you probably noted, the fourth verse of this psalm reads a little differently from the way Paul quoted it. The margin of my Bible has a footnote next to the word *tremble* which says, "with anger or fear." *And* could
be translated *but*. Thus it might read, "Tremble with anger, but do not
sin." Apparently the person is so filled with anger, so inflamed or burning,

that it causes him to tremble. I can understand that because there have been times when I have been so angry I was shaking just from inward agitation.

How does one handle the depth of anger? The psalmist gives us the solution.

3. From reading the psalm, what do you think the psalmist is going through? Is his anger justified or unjustified?

4. What is the psalmist's confidence in the midst of this distress?

5. What does he say to do in the midst of this shaking anger?

6. What can you learn from this psalm that you can apply to your life? Be as specific and personal as possible.

7. Look at Ephesians 4:31-32:

   Let all bitterness and wrath and anger and clamor and slander be put away from you, along with all malice. And be kind to one another, tenderhearted, forgiving each other, just as God in Christ also has forgiven you.

   a. What do you learn about your response to anger and wrath in these verses?

   b. How do you think verse 32 relates, if at all, to verse 31?

8. Read Colossians 3:8-17. How do these verses compare with the ones in Ephesians 4?

9. Now then, let's also take a look at Galatians 5:19-21:

Now the deeds of the flesh are evident, which are: immorality, impurity, sensuality, idolatry, sorcery, enmities, strife, jealousy, outburst of anger, disputes, dissensions, factions, envying, drunkenness, carousing, and things like these, of which I forewarn you just as I have forewarned you that those who practice such things shall not inherit the kingdom of God.

a. According to these verses, is anger always bad? Is it always a deed of the flesh? Read the passage carefully before you answer. Explain why you answer as you do.

b. Have you noticed the end of those who habitually practice these deeds as part of their lifestyles? What is it? What does this tell you about outbursts of anger?

10. Finally, I want you to look at James 1:19-26 again. Read it carefully and then answer the questions that follow.

This you know, my beloved brethren. But let everyone be quick to hear, slow to speak and slow to anger; for the anger of man does not achieve the righteousness of God. Therefore putting aside all filthiness and all that remains of wickedness, in humility receive the word implanted, which is able to save your souls. But prove yourselves doers of the word, and not merely hearers who delude themselves. For if anyone is a hearer of the word and not a doer, he is like a man who looks at his natural face in a mirror; for once he has looked at himself and gone away, he has immediately forgotten what kind of person he was. But one who looks intently at the perfect law, the law of liberty, and abides by it, not having become a forgetful hearer but an effectual doer, this man shall be blessed in what he does. If anyone thinks himself to be religious, and yet does not bridle his tongue but deceives his own heart, this man's religion is worthless.

a. What is God's command regarding anger?

b. What else does this passage say we are to do?

c. Could any of these other admonitions or exhortations help us handle our anger? How?

d. Why are you to control your anger?

Now then, let me summarize what you can do when you feel anger. When you feel anger:

1. *Turn from it. Don't let it control you. Be angry and sin not.* Proverbs 29:8,11 says, "Scorners set a city aflame, but wise men turn away anger.... A fool always loses his temper, but a wise man holds it back." Ecclesiastes 7:9 says, "Do not be eager in your heart [the footnote says this phrase can be translated "hasty in your spirit"] to be angry, for anger resides in the bosom of fools." Proverbs 16:32 reminds me of my husband, "He who is slow to anger is better than the mighty, and he who rules his spirit, than he who captures a city."

2. *Be willing to overlook others' transgressions against you.* This is meekness, not weakness. "A man's discretion makes him slow to anger, and it is his glory to overlook a transgression.... A man of great anger shall bear the penalty, for if you rescue him, you will only have to do it again" (Proverbs 19:11,19).

3. *When people say or do something which makes you angry, give them a gentle answer.* "A gentle answer turns away wrath, but a harsh word stirs up anger" (Proverbs 15:1). A harsh word can not only stir up anger in them, it can also stir up anger in you!

4. *Deal with your feelings. Don't just stuff them down.* "Meditate in your heart upon your bed, and be still. Offer the sacrifices of righteousness, and trust in the LORD" (Psalm 4:4-5). In other words, think through your anger, bring your feelings to the Word of God, and then determine that you are going to sacrifice those emotions and desires for

the sake of righteousness. As you read through the psalms, you will find the psalmist over and over again dealing with his emotions, telling God how he feels, and then remembering truth and acting accordingly. Watch for this. I think it will bless you.

5. *Trust in the Lord.* How well Psalm 37 has taught us this. Remember the story of Joseph in the Old Testament. If anyone could justify anger, it would have been Joseph. However, Joseph was never ruled by anger. What he knew, you need to remember: "And as for you, you meant evil against me, but God meant it for good in order to bring about this present result, to preserve many people alive" (Genesis 50:20). Whatever you go through, if you will handle it as Joseph did, you will find God giving you a ministry that will help preserve others.

6. *"Never take your own revenge,* beloved, but leave room for the wrath of God, for it is written, 'VENGEANCE IS MINE, I WILL REPAY,' says the Lord" (Roman 12:19).

Because I don't want you to miss anything that God has for you in this study, I want to ask you to do one more thing. List what God has shown you personally in today's study. What verses have specifically spoken to you in regard to the way you deal with anger?

Look up 1 Peter 5:6-7 and write these verses out.

Take the next few minutes and pray these verses back to the Lord. Let them be your heart's cry as you humble yourself under the mighty hand of your Father God. Confess your anger to Him, and agree with Him that it is sin. Turn from that anger and forsake it, casting all your anxiety, anger, bitterness, hurt on Him who loves you so.

Now, look back over your study on anger. Review the truths that you have gleaned. Write out a prayer of commitment to the Lord.

MEMORY VERSE

Humble yourselves, therefore, under the mighty hand of God, that He may exalt you at the proper time, casting all your anxiety upon Him, because He cares for you.

1 PETER 5:6-7

SMALL-GROUP DISCUSSION QUESTIONS

In week eleven we looked at the fact that people can be healed from the wounds of their past if they will come to God on His terms and be willing to be healed His way.

We have seen that healing is a matter of faith—not anything else. It's up to us to believe or not to believe, to obey or not to obey. It's our choice —opportunity by opportunity, moment by moment.

We also talked about why some people do not want to be healed. Then we looked at our responsibility in forgiving others and the results of forgiveness.

1. It could be that your healing has not been complete because there is anger in your life. This week as you studied anger, did you deal with any anger that is still in your heart? If not, why? What is keeping you from letting go?

2. You saw in your study that God gets angry.
   a. What kind of anger is this?
   b. What are the things that anger God?
   c. What is the root cause of the things that anger God?
   d. What did you learn about God's anger?
3. What are the two kinds of anger that man experiences?
   a. Is anger against God ever justified?
   b. What are some of the reasons man gets angry with God?
   c. What did you see in Isaiah 45:20-24 that would help you deal with anger against God?
   d. What are some of the responses that cause us to get angry with people?
   e. What two things did you learn about responding to anger in Ephesians 4:26? What did you learn in Ephesians 4:31-32?
   f. In Psalm 4 we saw that the psalmist was very angry with people. What was his confidence in the midst of his situation? What did you learn from this psalm about dealing with your anger toward people?
   g. Have you ever been angry at the wicked?
   h. What did you learn in Psalm 37 that would help you in handling this anger?
4. What can be the results of anger when it is not released to God and dealt with properly?
5. What will unreleased anger eventually lead to?
6. You studied Galatians 5:19-21.
   a. Is anger always bad?
   b. Is anger always a deed of the flesh?
   c. What is the end of those who habitually practice the deeds listed in this passage?
   d. In light of your last response, what does that tell you about outbursts of anger?
7. What is God's command regarding anger in James 1:19-26?

a. How do these admonitions and exhortations help us handle anger?

b. Why are you to control your anger?

8. Now in your own words, explain what you are to do when you are angry.

9. Will you rest in the Lord and cease from anger? What have you determined before the Lord to do the next time you feel anger rising in your heart?

13

THE CURE FOR BITTERNESS

— D A Y   O N E —

Meekness will open the iron doors that have held you captive in a cell of anger and bitterness. It's the key. Meekness grants you a peace and freedom like you have never experienced before.

Meekness is an attitude of submission and trust that accepts all of God's ways with us as good and therefore does not murmur, dispute, or retaliate.[1] It realizes that what comes to us from man is permitted and used by God for our discipline as His children and thus for purifying us. Meekness is a trusting attitude that looks beyond circumstances and beyond man to the sovereign God and, bowing the knee, says, "Lord, what pleases Thee pleases me."

From that description, it is obvious that meekness is not the natural disposition of sinful man, nor is true meekness possible apart from the Spirit of God. Because meekness is an inwrought grace of the soul, it is only possible when Jesus Christ lives within. It is our Lord who is meek and lowly in heart.[2]

Psalm 37:11 says, "But the humble will inherit the land, and will delight themselves in abundant prosperity." Another word for humble is *meek*. How well this verse in Psalm 37 parallels Jesus' words in the Sermon on the Mount when He says, "Blessed are the meek, for they shall inherit the earth" (Matthew 5:5, KJV).

I don't believe there is a person born who does not have within his or her heart some hope, some dream of a life of fulfillment and enjoyment— a desire to receive all that life has to offer. "Inherit the land" is a way to describe this "hope." It parallels "inheriting the earth"—the earth, which is the Lord's and the fullness thereof.

Read through Psalm 37 and mark each verse which speaks of *inheriting the earth*. As you do, you will come up with a wonderful description of those who are meek. Write out what you see.

In Psalm 37:9 we see it is those who wait for the Lord who inherit the land. One of the characteristics of meekness is trust. You may have suffered greatly in this life. You may seem deprived in the world's eyes, and possibly in your own, but there is a life for you yet unseen, yet unexperienced, which is so wonderful "that the sufferings of this present time are not worthy to be compared with the glory that is to be revealed to us" (Romans 8:18). Abundant life awaits. The wicked will perish—vanish (Psalm 37:20), but you will inherit the land.

In Psalm 37:18 we read, "The LORD knows the days of the blameless; and their inheritance will be forever." You are made blameless in Christ Jesus. You walk a blameless life by being filled with, and controlled by, the Spirit. And part of the fruit of the Spirit is meekness (Galatians 5:23— translated *gentleness* in the NASB).

In Psalm 37:22,29 we see that it's the blessed and the righteous who inherit the land—that's the meek.

Meekness is the attitude which trusts, commits, rests, and waits in the Lord. That's what Psalm 37 is all about. And the reward for such a spirit is given in Psalm 37:34: "Wait for the LORD, and keep His way, and He will exalt you to inherit the land; when the wicked are cut off, you will see it."

"The posterity of the wicked will be cut off. But the salvation of the righteous is from the LORD; He is their strength in time of trouble. And the LORD helps them, and delivers them; He delivers them from the wicked, and saves them, because they take refuge in Him" (Psalm 37:38-40).

You need not hold on to your anger. You need not seek to get even with your perpetrators, Beloved. In meekness, let go of it all. Lay it at the feet of your Savior. Take refuge in Him. Draw from His strength. Know the awesome, incredible release and peace of letting all anger and bitterness go. The Lord will help you. Don't worry about revenge! In righteousness He will deal with those who have sinned against you or your loved ones. Don't let your anger destroy you. What a victory this would give to the wicked! Put anger and bitterness away by clothing yourself in His meekness.

When anger hits, meekness will bring it under control. When you walk in meekness, you turn the other cheek. "Love your enemies, and pray for those who persecute you in order that you may be sons of your Father who is in heaven; for He causes His sun to rise on the evil and the good, and sends rain on the righteous and the unrighteous.... Therefore you are to be perfect, as your heavenly Father is perfect" (Matthew 5:39,44-45,48).

Meekness can behave in this manner because it realizes that the insults and the injuries which man may inflict are only permitted and used by God for the chastening and purifying of His child.

Come to Him, you who are weary and heavy-laden with hurt, anger, and bitterness, and He will give you rest. Take His yoke upon you—become His partner. Make the kingdom of God and its glory your goal, your task. Learn from Jesus, for He is meek and humble in heart. You will then find rest—blessed, sweet rest for your souls. You will find His yoke easy and pleasant and His load light—light because you are yoked together with the omnipotent One who is your burden bearer.

Bow your knees in prayer. Take the definition of meekness and personalize it. Tell God you will accept His dealings with you as good, and, therefore, you will stop murmuring about your past. You will quit disputing with Him over why these things happened. You will exchange your anger and your bitterness for His meekness. Tell Him that you will trust Him to use the horrible and difficult things of your life as His instruments of discipline and purification to make you into the image of His Son.

– D A Y   T W O –

Bitterness comes when you don't respond to the difficult circumstances of life from a biblical perspective. It is an angry and resentful state of mind that can often be directed toward God. Such bitterness causes a person to despise God's blessings. Bitterness can also be toward man, manifesting its presence as an angry and hostile outlook on life expressed in resentment and outbursts on others.

If bitterness is not released and forsaken, it will trouble the soil of the heart where it will grow. And it will produce fruit which troubles the life in which it has taken root. It will also defile others.

The passage which teaches you how to deal with bitterness is Hebrews 12. In order to appreciate Hebrews 12, you need to understand the context and occasion of this epistle.

Hebrews is a word of exhortation written to Hebrew Christians undergoing a great testing of their faith. They had endured a "great conflict of sufferings, partly, by being made a public spectacle through reproaches and tribulations, and partly by becoming sharers with those who were so treated" (Hebrews 10:32-33). Some had been imprisoned because of their faith. Others had suffered loss of property and possessions simply because they were Christians. Many had suffered ill-treatment. For some, the temptation to forsake their newfound Christianity and return to the old covenant style of worship was very strong. Christianity was a discipline of life which cost greatly, and some were wondering if it was worth it.

The purpose of Hebrews 12 is to encourage these suffering saints to "lay aside every encumbrance, and the sin which so easily entangles us, and…run with endurance the race that is set before us, fixing our eyes on Jesus" (verses 1-2). After saying all of this and then setting before them the example of Jesus Christ, the author of Hebrews explains the nature of what they are enduring. It is the *paideia* of the Lord—the child training, the discipline, which all true children of God experience.

Read Hebrews 12:5-15 so that you can see what bitterness has to do with discipline. As you read, mark each use of the word *discipline*. Also mark the words *son* and *children* in the same way. Mark too the pronouns that relate to us, His children: *your, we,* and *our.* Mark the words *grace* and *bitterness* and each reference to the *Lord,* along with the pronouns which refer to Him.

● HEBREWS 12:5-15

5 And you have forgotten the exhortation which is addressed to you as sons, "MY SON, DO NOT REGARD LIGHTLY THE DISCIPLINE OF THE LORD, NOR FAINT WHEN YOU ARE REPROVED BY HIM;

6 FOR THOSE WHOM THE LORD LOVES HE DISCIPLINES, AND HE SCOURGES EVERY SON WHOM HE RECEIVES."

7 It is for discipline that you endure; God deals with you as with sons; for what son is there whom his father does not discipline?

8 But if you are without discipline, of which all have become partakers, then you are illegitimate children and not sons.

9 Furthermore, we had earthly fathers to discipline us, and we respected them; shall we not much rather be subject to the Father of spirits, and live?

10 For they disciplined us for a short time as seemed best to them, but He disciplines us for our good, that we may share His holiness.

11 All discipline for the moment seems not to be joyful, but sorrowful; yet to those who have been trained by it, afterwards it yields the peaceful fruit of righteousness.

12 Therefore, strengthen the hands that are weak and the knees that are feeble,

13 and make straight paths for your feet, so that the limb which is lame may not be put out of joint, but rather be healed.

14 Pursue peace with all men, and the sanctification without which no one will see the Lord.

15 See to it that no one comes short of the grace of God; that no root of bitterness springing up causes trouble, and by it many be defiled.

Now then, make a list of everything you learned about each word that you marked. Make sure you don't miss any instructions or commands which are given to us.

Finally, write out a brief statement explaining how all of these truths relate to the healing of hurts. What in this passage would cure your anger and bitterness and would keep you from being victimized by the events of your life?

My friend, this study is very important. Do you realize how imperative it is that you embrace these truths and live accordingly? There will not be any true, deep, and lasting healing apart from such obedience of faith.

— D A Y   T H R E E —

Acceptance is one of the primary contingencies upon which your healing rests. I said *acceptance*—not *acquiescence*. To accept is to believe and to submit. To acquiesce is simply to give in, to resign yourself to something or someone.

What must you accept if you are to be healed by the Lord? The following list captures what *I believe* is essential—crucial—mandatory for healing.

1. *Know God—accept His character and His sovereignty.* Why are we to accept His sovereignty? If God is not in charge—totally and completely— then whose hands are we in? If He were unaware of what was going to happen to us, then how could He work all things together for our good and our Christlikeness? Surely if man, Satan, accidents, or "fate" can do things to us without God's permission or knowledge, then we are in grave trouble because it would mean that God is not in charge.

Because God is sovereign, you need to know what this God is like who rules over all. One of the primary attributes of God a hurting person needs to understand is that of love. God loves you, my friend, no matter what you are like, no matter what you do. God is love, and it is His love that draws you to Him. He initiates love.

God says, "I have loved you with an everlasting love; therefore I have drawn you with lovingkindness" (Jeremiah 31:3). Love desires your highest good and is willing to pay the ultimate of sacrifices to attain it. That sacrifice was His Son. Hurts are healed by unconditional love. Accept His love. Accept His character. Accept His sovereignty.

2. *Accept the grace of God.* There is a threefold aspect to the grace of God which affects your healing.

First, you must accept the saving grace of God because it is by grace that you are saved through faith. Grace is a gift of God, never the result of works. In His covenant of grace God takes away your sins and puts His Spirit within you. The indwelling Spirit enables you to live a righteous life. The Spirit is also the seal, the guarantee, that God will keep and complete His covenant by redeeming your body and granting you life eternal in His presence.

When you accept the grace of God, you accept the fact that Jesus is God, the One who will deliver you from your sin as you acknowledge that He is who He says He is and, therefore, that He has the right to rule your life. Over and over again in our counseling, my staff and I have seen that accepting and submitting to the deity, to the lordship of Jesus Christ, is essential to healing.

Second, grace keeps you from bitterness. Let's look more closely at Hebrews 12:15-16: "See to it that no one comes short of the grace of God; that no root of bitterness springing up causes trouble, and by it many be defiled; that there be no immoral or godless person like Esau, who sold his own birthright for a single meal."

In the midst of trials, of testing, of temptation, you can rest assured that God's grace is sufficient to allow you to handle anything which comes your way. In His sovereignty when your heavenly Father allows you to endure discipline or to experience chastenings of your child-training, you are not to come short of the grace of God by failing to appropriate everything which God has provided for you and which is freely given to you on one condition and on one condition only: the condition of faith.

The author of Hebrews uses Esau as an example of one who failed to appropriate God's grace. In a moment of extreme physical hunger, Esau despised his birthright in order to gain the temporary satisfaction of his flesh. God's grace was sufficient to help Esau handle his cravings, but Esau did not appropriate it.

Do you see the parallel? God's grace is sufficient for any trial, any hurt, any failure. It is yours unconditionally, for the mere believing. The question is, Will you appropriate it in faith? Whatever your hurt, your wound, your past, His grace is sufficient. *Accept His grace.*

The third aspect of His grace which you need to accept for your healing is in respect to who and what you are. Paul said in 1 Corinthians 15:10, "But by the grace of God I am what I am." Everything from the time of your conception to right now has gone into that which has made you His and, thus, His co-laborer for the furtherance of His kingdom. This truth may be hard for you to comprehend, but this is what God's Word says, and God does not lie.

Remember John 15:16: "You did not choose Me, but I chose you, and appointed you, that you should go and bear fruit, and that your fruit should remain, that whatever you ask of the Father in My name, He may give to you." You are God's "workmanship, created in Christ Jesus unto good works, which God hath before ordained" for you to walk in (Ephesians 2:10, KJV).

For you to fail to accept these truths and live in faithful obedience to them is to come short of the grace of God. Paul never allowed the sinfulness of his past, the incarceration and subsequent death of Christians, the timing of his salvation, his unattractive appearance and speech, or his less-than-perfect performance as a Christian to keep him from going forward to a fruitful life for Christ. Because Paul accepted the grace of God in all its fullness, he was able to say, "His grace toward me did not prove vain; but I labored even more than all of them, yet not I, but the grace of God with me" (1 Corinthians 15:10).

For God's grace to prove vain in your life is to say, "I know what God is saying, BUT _____." Whatever you would add here would contradict the veracity of His Word and the sufficiency of His grace because His grace takes your weakness and transforms it into His strength.

My friend, do you realize that God does not need anything you have? He wants only who you are so that He can fill you with Himself.

As you move out in faith, accepting His grace, your life will have great significance in His kingdom. Many times its significance may remain unseen to you, but it is not unseen to God. It is all a matter of faith's obedience. Grace will do the rest. Now then, do not let His grace be in vain—accept it.

3. *Accept God's love.* Love heals. We will study this truth for the next two days. But for today, go to the Lord and ask Him to show you if you are failing in any of these areas we've discussed. Then, in the space which follows, write down what God shows you and what you need to do about it.

Unbelief, which is the root of all sin, is cured by belief—and belief brings healing.

— D A Y   F O U R —

God loves you with an everlasting, unconditional love. When you accept that truth and cling to it no matter what, you will find healing. Dorie, my dear friend, illustrates this well. When I first met Dorie Van Stone, she and I shared the platform at a conference given at Moody Bible Institute.

Dorie was one of two daughters—"the ugly one," Dorie says. Rejected by her mother while her sister was welcomed with open arms, Dorie was placed in an orphanage where she was beaten every single night. All sorts of abuse, including sexual abuse, went on in that orphanage, but it was there that Dorie first heard from a visiting church group that God loved her. Although she never felt love from anyone, in childlike faith Dorie accepted the fact that God loved her.

Clutching the gift of her own New Testament and that one truth, Dorie endured years of much physical and emotional abuse. From the orphanage, Dorie was put in a foster home where she was nothing but a despised slave. It was believing God loved her that held her through the total rejection of her mother. Brought before a court to claim her child, Dorie's mom refused to take custody of her, telling the judge in Dorie's presence she wished Dorie had never been born. Believing the truth of God's love held Dorie through the joy of finding her father, experiencing his love, and then being rejected by him because of her refusal to deny Jesus Christ. Believing God's love and sovereignty held Dorie through the sudden and unexpected death of her husband, Lloyd, at the age of sixty-two.

Read Dorie's book, *Dorie: The Girl Nobody Loved*, listen to her testimony on tape,[3] and you will hear a living testimony of love's power to heal.

Today, there are many voices in the world, and even in Christendom, telling us that the root source of our problems is a lack of self-love and self-esteem. It sounds good, especially when it comes from the so-called experts. It may even sound more plausible when it comes from active Christians. It also seems more credible when we see it in print—discussed, explained, and substantiated by other "experts" in magazines and books. But what does the Word of God say about self-esteem, self-worth, our self-image? Nothing except that apart from Jesus we are nothing.

Nowhere does the Word of God tell us that our problem is lack of self-esteem or lack of self-love or a poor self-image. Instead, the Bible tells us that from the very beginning of the Garden of Eden, man's problem was unbelief. Unbelief, as you have already seen, caused man to sin. Sin separated man from God, and God is love. When man cuts himself off from love, he then begins the search to find a substitute. In this search, many hurts are incurred, many wounds inflicted. Self-love is that poor, but very deluding, substitute of God's love that deceptively puts man at the center instead of God. It is then that God exists for man, rather than man for God.

Self-love and self-esteem will teach you that you have worth and value apart from God. That is pride. It is the devil's lie! Some will tell you that before you can love God or man, you must have healthy self-love and self-esteem. Or they will tell you that you can never love your neighbor until you love yourself.

These are subtle distortions of the Word of God. They are distortions that you can buy into unsuspectingly if you do not stop and examine them carefully. I even found myself reading the books, listening to the tapes, and picking up the jargon of some who love God and who are being acclaimed as experts. Because people flock to listen to them and are helped to some degree, it does not mean they are teaching the truth. Although some are seemingly healed, it does not make the method or theory right or pleasing in the eyes of God. People are healed through psychic surgery, but that doesn't make it right. However, in the teaching of self-love and self-esteem, you can be subtly deceived. These words and teachings are just a shade away from truth, but a shade that will lead you further from the warmth of the Son into greater chilling darkness.

Acceptance of love is crucial to your healing, but it is acceptance of God's love rather than self-love. When you don't like who you are or what you have done, or when the enemy comes whispering in your ear, knocking at the door of your mind, telling you that you are nothing, agree with your adversary. Then give him the truth. Tell him that apart from Jesus Christ you are nothing and you can do nothing that has any eternal worth or value.

Also tell Satan that God loves you when you are nothing, accepts you just the way you are, and loves you with an everlasting, unconditional love that is in the process of transforming you into His image. Tell the devil that you are secure in God's love "because the love of God has been poured out within" your heart "through the Holy Spirit who was given to us" (Romans 5:5), and nothing "shall be able to separate [you] from the love of God, which is in Christ Jesus our Lord" (Romans 8:39).

Martin Luther had it right when he said, "God does not love us because we are valuable, but we are valuable because God loves us." "In this is love, not that we loved God, but that He loved us and sent His Son to be the propitiation for our sins. Beloved, if God so loved us, we also ought to love one another.... If we love one another, God abides in us, and His love is perfected in us" (1 John 4:10-12).

— D A Y   F I V E —

When you accept God's love, you will allow God to love others through you. This is part of healing.

Having believed and received the love of God and, thus, having His love poured out within our hearts, we then become channels for His love (Romans 5:5). And the healing goes on. "We love, because He first loved us" (1 John 4:19).

How different from what we're hearing! So many are saying that self-love is the prerequisite for loving others. They say our ability to love God and to love our neighbor is proportionate to our ability to love ourselves. In other words, if you can't love yourself, you can't love your neighbor or God.

The way to love others is not through love of self. In order to really love God and others, we must die to self. Death to self causes me to take up my cross, deny myself, and follow Him.

1. Look up Mark 8:35-36. What is Jesus saying about our lives in these verses?

2. What does Paul say regarding self in Galatians 2:20?

   a. Write out Galatians 2:20 and begin memorizing it.

   b. Now that you have written it out, how does this compare with what I've said about self-love/self-esteem/self-image?

As you and I learn to live the crucified life, it will continually be death to self rather than love of self. Are you asking, "But what about the command to love my neighbor as myself? Doesn't this mean I am to love myself?" Let's do a little investigation in the Word so you can have God's answer.

3. Look up Romans 13:8-10 and write out the verses.

4. Now read Mark 12:28-33.

5. In either of these passages is God telling you or commanding you to love yourself? What is He teaching about self in these verses?

6. Look up Philippians 2:3-8. Does this teach love of self or death to self? What, in essence, are these verses saying that would help us have a proper biblical opinion regarding self? As you answer this, do not miss Christ's example.

7. Now look up 2 Timothy 3:1-5. What do you learn in respect to love of self in this passage?

Some who support the view of self-love and self-esteem point to the cross as a testimony of our worth and value. They say that if we did not have worth, God would not have died for us.

O Beloved, *the cross does not demonstrate our worth to God; it demonstrates God's unconditional love toward us.*

The Bible says, "God so loved the world, that He gave His only begotten Son." It *does not say* that God so esteemed or saw the value of man that He gave His only begotten Son. A careful study of Romans, especially chapter 9, will show us that God is never obligated to man. Rather, it was in mercy God saved us. "So then He has mercy on whom He desires, and He hardens whom He desires" (9:18). Salvation is pure and total grace—it therefore cannot be based on worth.

Please, please, when you present the gospel, don't present it on the basis of man's worth, for you would distort it. It is pure grace that pours out love "that saved a wretch like me," as John Newton, the writer of "Amazing Grace," so well worded it. "It is a trustworthy statement, deserving full acceptance, that Christ Jesus came into the world to save sinners, among whom I am foremost of all. And yet for this reason I found mercy" (1 Timothy 1:15-16). Sinners deserve hell. God in love, mercy, and grace offers us heaven, a place and life where He will eternally express His love for us. A place where, at last, we will be able to fully express ours for Him...because He first loved us!

Will you not only accept His love, but will you accept your calling— the cross—where you died to self, that you might live for God? You will become a channel for His love to others. You will, as a branch, bear the fruit of love, not for self, but for others. His love flowing through you will heal others.

– D A Y   S I X –

Written at the top of the yellow legal pad were these words: "Use whatever you want, whenever you need to. May God be glorified through all of this." And so for His glory, I have chosen the following:

I never knew what maternal or paternal love was truly like. My parents were raised in homes where love was not expressed, and, consequently, we—my two brothers and one sister—were also raised this way. Of the four children, I seemed to be the one that was selected to be picked on. I was also the caretaker—I held everyone else together. I seemed to sense the rejection and lack of love, because at a very early age I began to try to destroy myself. This pattern lasted until I came to the Lord at thirty years of age.

Fired at with a shotgun by a drunken father, she was the maid, the cook, the housekeeper for her alcoholic parents and her siblings. She was the rescuer of her mother when her father would abusively rape her in a drunken rage. Sexually molested by her grandfather from the age of ten, she wrote:

I grew to hate sex because of the perverted way I saw it used. Now I saw it used in another way and grew to hate it even more. When my grand-father would take advantage of me, I was like a corpse. I was so full of fear. I became fearful of all men and became even more isolated. He had progressed from touching to intercourse, and I had digressed from being an innocent child to being an adult in a child's body. I felt abused in every way. To me, this was a fate worse than death. I was being tormented by the very people who were supposed to love and nurture me into adulthood. I felt like no one cared. I became a very angry child and began to act out my behavior in delinquent ways. I was so desperately looking for someone to care, but it seemed that no one did. God did—but at this point I had no idea who He really was. I had only heard His name in cursing, not as my Father or as Someone Who cared about what happened to me. I got into serious trouble with the law for breaking into a house and stealing things.

Eventually in the sovereignty of God, through a bus ministry, this woman was exposed to God's people. What a lesson there is for us in tirelessly expressing God's unconditional love to others as she writes: "God brought many people into my life to draw me to Himself. I searched and searched but would never trust enough to totally let go and allow God to run my life. As soon as my parents noticed how much I enjoyed church, that was taken away."

At the age of seventeen, after a severe beating by her dad, she was placed in a foster home. "God knew what He was doing. They were neat Christian people." But "I ran away from anyone that required a commitment. Life became unbearable again." She attempted suicide, but it was to get attention. A year of Bible school followed, with a godly couple taking a vested interest in her. After graduating from college with a degree in psychology, "I was still searching for the answer. I tried so hard to figure out why I was having problems."

With all the psychology and head knowledge from the Bible, I still had no peace. In the meantime, I got involved in Precept and started studying with a fervor. I wanted so much to know Who God was and what purpose my life was to have. I began teaching emotionally disturbed children in school and drowned out my problems by helping them. I became even more depressed and suicidal. I shut all of my friends out. They would call me on the phone, but I would let it ring for hours. They would come over, and I would not go to the door. I began to reject anyone that tried to help. The old pattern had taken over again. I STILL HAD NOT DIED TO MYSELF. I wanted to run my life and let God have a little of it. A friend came over one evening and met me at the door as I was leaving.

She backed me into the living room and sat down and tried to explain to me what I was doing to her and my other friends. It had never occurred to me that I was hurting anyone but myself. They really cared about me, but I did not believe them. My friend started crying, and I could not believe it. I had never had anyone cry over anything I had done to myself. It blew me away.

After she left I really began to examine my heart. It was stone cold. God so convicted me and showed me my sin and just how selfish I really was. I decided then and there that it was time to let go and allow Him to totally control my life. I felt such a peace. The depression lifted, but the old patterns were hard to break. Through losing my job, I saw that my devotion is to be to Him totally. When I put other things before Him, He will weed them out and show me where my true devotion is to be.

God has so changed my life. I no longer have to live under depression or with suicidal thoughts. THE CHOICE IS MINE. I am dead and no longer have to live that way. It has become a joy to live in freedom because I know that in and through Christ I can do anything that God requires of me.

I still have to deal with the rejection, but I know God is there. He is, and was, in control and will not allow anything into my life that is not for my good, that is not for His glory, or that I cannot handle with His help. He is God! Who am I to question what He is doing? "Therefore in Christ Jesus I have found reason for boasting in things pertaining to God. For I will not presume to speak of anything except what Christ has accomplished through me" (Romans 15:17-18).

There is a vital lesson in this testimony which you must not miss, and that is the constant need to cast all your care upon God. While I have not named every hurt you may have to deal with, basically the cure will be found, in principle, in what we have covered and in what will be covered tomorrow. Every time a hurt arises, a pain occurs, a memory is triggered, humble yourself before God. Do not try to deal with it in your own strength or in your way. Jesus is there. You are yoked to Him. Roll that burden, that care, that anxiety, over onto His shoulders. He cares for you (1 Peter 5:6-7).

– D A Y   S E V E N –

Many of our hurts center around a lack of acceptance. Do you remember the hurt you have felt when others have not accepted you for what you were? The hurt which came when others, in one way or another, rejected you? We're hurt *because we are not accepted by others;* and so we feel rejected. We also experience hurt *because we do not accept others.*

We will deal with the second aspect of hurt, not accepting others, in our final day of study.

People hurt because their parents, their husband or wife, their children, their friends, someone in their life, did not live up to or meet their expectations, desires, or ideals.

Let me summarize it this way. Generally we hurt and find it difficult to accept people:

1. because we feel (rightly or wrongly) that they owe us something, a "debt" they have not fulfilled—maybe love, respect, honor, time.

2. because they are not what we wanted or expected in our relationship with them, e.g., as a father, mother, daughter, son, husband, wife, friend.

3. because in their actions, their mannerisms, or their treatment of us, they remind us of someone who has hurt us, embittered us, failed us, or rejected us.

In other words, our hurt has come because we were the ones unable to accept others for one of the reasons I just mentioned. For instance, maybe you hurt because you never had the *Leave It to Beaver* or the *Father Knows Best* type of family life that you saw portrayed weekly on television while you were growing up.

Or you watched *The Cosby Show* and just withered inside because your dad was never around, and if he was, he didn't want to be bothered with you. Maybe you even went to him and begged him for more attention. Maybe you told him there was a deep void in your life because he didn't hold you, touch you, wrestle with you, go to your games or school activities, or simply be and do what a father is to be and do. Maybe you got up the courage to express all of this, and still he didn't change. When that happens, the hurt seems even worse, for it is not as if he doesn't know your needs. Now he knows and still doesn't care or doesn't do anything about it. In a sense it is an even worse rejection.

Then if people come along and tell you that because you have been deprived of your father's love and attention you are going to have problems for the rest of your life, your hurt intensifies. How depressing! How defeating! And it will be, Beloved, continually, hauntingly defeating until you accept your father just the way he is. The hurt and pain will continue, not because he hasn't accepted you, but because you have not accepted him just the way he is. Your father's rejection of you, his unwillingness to meet your needs as his child, his lack of selfless love, is wrong. He will stand accountable to the heavenly Father. However, you cannot change him. What you can change is your response to your father—no one else can do it for you.

Healing won't come until you bow before God in meekness and accept the fact that this relationship has been permitted by God and has an eternal purpose. If that relationship would have permanently damaged you as many caught in worldly wisdom would say, then God would have divinely intervened. Remember—never forget—God's Word promises that all things will work together for your good to conform you to His image. Never forget you are beloved to Him.

I have used the illustration of a parent and child; however, as I am sure you realize, we could use other combinations of people, such as husband and wife, you and…whomever.

Now then, I want you to take a few minutes to think about those individuals who trouble you in some way—those who irritate you, those you want to shun, those whom you don't want to have anything to do with at all.

1. Make a list of their names. Then, considering the following five questions, write out the answers to those which are pertinent to each person. It may be best to make your list on a separate sheet of paper.
   a. What do you think _____ owes you?
   b. What do you deserve in your relationship with _____ that you are not receiving or have never received?

c. Is the mold that you expect him/her to fit into one that you are sure God expects?

d. Do you resent that person because he or she reminds you of someone? Who? How?

e. Do you project feelings, attitudes, or thoughts on that person that you are not absolutely sure he or she has? Why?

2. In what state were you, my friend, when Jesus Christ accepted you? If you were to extend the love of God to the people you listed, how would you respond to each of them? List their names, and then next to each, write out what you need to do *to* or *with* each in order to be obedient.

3. Are you willing to forgive them? Remember love and forgiveness go together as do two ears, two nostrils, two eyes.

4. Now go back through your list of names and one by one tell God you will, in an act of faithful obedience, accept them as He and His Son have accepted them.

I cannot believe our thirteen weeks are complete. Thank you for hanging in there and for diligently studying God's Word. I'm sure you realize, my friend, that merely knowing all these truths and principles will not bring about your healing. They must be applied moment by moment, opportunity by opportunity. If you cannot do that alone, do not be ashamed. God did not leave you alone. He made you a part of His body. Ask your Father God to direct you to someone who knows the Word, who loves the Lord, and who will come alongside you to walk you through the truths of God's Word which need application in your life.

And above all, do not let this be the end of your Bible study. I have been praying that you will get into a systematic study of God's Word. There are many good Bible studies available to Christians today. I would suggest you choose one which will teach you to dig into God's Word on your own so that you learn skills which will enable you to study and discern truth by yourself. I believe difficult days are ahead, and God's people need to know how to feed themselves. Of course, I would count it a privilege to continue to be your teacher in an indirect way through our Precept Upon Precept Bible Studies, our In and Out Bible Studies, through the *New Inductive Study Bible,* or the *International Inductive Study Series.*

An ongoing study in the Word is crucial as preventative medicine for the hurts of life which are bound to come. If the Word of God is the balm of Gilead, we cannot go without it! And it is!

May "grace and peace be multiplied to you in the knowledge of God and of Jesus our Lord; seeing that His divine power has granted to us everything pertaining to life and godliness, through the true knowledge of Him who called us by His own glory and excellence. For by these He has granted to us His precious and magnificent promises, in order that by them you might become partakers of the divine nature, having escaped the corruption that is in the world by lust" (2 Peter 1:2-4).

"For behold, the day is coming, burning like a furnace; and all the arrogant and every evildoer will be chaff; and the day that is coming will set them ablaze," says the LORD of hosts, "so that it will leave them neither root nor branch. But for you who fear My name the sun of righteousness will rise with healing in its wings; and you will go forth and skip about like calves from the stall. And you will tread down the wicked, for they shall be ashes under the soles of your feet on the day which I am preparing," says the LORD of hosts. (Malachi 4:1-3)

My heart is filled with His love for you.

MEMORY VERSE

I have been crucified with Christ; and it is no longer I who live, but Christ lives in me; and the life which I now live in the flesh I live by faith in the Son of God, who loved me, and delivered Himself up for me.

GALATIANS 2:20

SMALL-GROUP DISCUSSION QUESTIONS

In week twelve we looked at two kinds of anger—anger at man and anger at God. We talked about reasons why each of these kinds of anger might occur, and we studied passages that help us learn how to deal with our anger in a godly way.

1. What is the key to dealing with anger and bitterness?
2. What is your definition of meekness?
3. What causes us to become bitter? To whom is bitterness directed?
4. When we are bitter toward man, how is this bitterness expressed? If it is toward God, how is it manifested?
5. From your study of Hebrews 12, what did you learn that would help in the healing of your hurts and that would cure your anger and bitterness and keep you from being victimized by the events of your life?
   a. How does this passage show the relationship of bitterness and meekness?
   b. What was the occasion of the writing of Hebrews?

    c. What were the circumstances of those to whom this letter was written?

    d. What was involved in their testing, according to Hebrews 10:32-33?

    e. What were some of the things they had suffered?

    f. What was the result of this suffering?

    g. What was the message, the purpose of Hebrews 12?

6. According to Hebrews 12:5-7, how are we to view the discipline of the Lord?

7. In the midst of the trials and testings, you can rest assured that He knows it all and that His grace is sufficient. What did you learn about the grace of God?

8. We saw that acceptance of God's love is vital to healing. When you accept God's love, you will allow God to love others through you by dying to self and taking up the cross and following Him. In Mark 8:35-36, what does Jesus say about our lives?

9. Since you memorized Mark 8:35-36, tell what you know from this verse about self-love, self-esteem.

10. What did you learn from the Scriptures about a proper opinion of self?

11. Did Christ die for you because you were worthy? Why did He die for you? What is the message of the cross?

12. Another source of hurt is that we have not accepted others.

    a. Why do we find it difficult to accept others?

    b. How do we deal with these feelings so that we can be healed?

    c. How does accepting others tie in with meekness?

    d. What were you like when God first loved you? Do you have any reason not to accept and love others?

13. Are you willing to forgive? How has this week's lesson convicted you, and how have you responded?

14. You may want to finish this study by having a time of praise, testimony, worship—even around a covered-dish dinner, a luncheon, or whatever is appropriate to your group. It would be good to let people share what this study has meant to them and how they would like the group to uphold them in prayer.

ATTRIBUTES OF GOD

Omniscient—God knows all. He has a perfect knowledge of everything that is past, present, or future. Job 37:16; Psalm 139:1-6

Omnipotent—God possesses all power. He is able to bring into being anything that He has decided to do, with or without the use of any means. Genesis 18:14; Job 42:2; Jeremiah 32:27.

Omnipresent—God is present everywhere, in all the universe, at all times, in the totality of His character. Proverbs 15:3; Jeremiah 23:23-24.

Eternal—God has no beginning, and He has no end. He is not confined to the finiteness of time or of man's reckoning of time. He is, in fact, the cause of time. Deuteronomy 32:40; Isaiah 57:15.

Immutable—God is always the same in His nature, His character, and His will. He never changes, and He can never be made to change. Psalm 102:25-27; Malachi 3:6; Hebrews 13:8.

Incomprehensible—Because God is God, He is beyond the understanding of man. His ways, character, and acts are higher than ours. We only understand as He chooses to reveal. Job 11:7; Isaiah 55:8-9; Romans 11:33.

Self-existent—There is nothing upon which God depends for His existence except Himself. The whole basis of His existence is within Himself. There was a time when there was nothing but God Himself. He added nothing to Himself by creation. Exodus 3:14; John 5:26.

Self-sufficient—Within Himself, God is able to act—to bring about His will without any assistance. Although He may choose to use assistance, it is His choice, not His need. Psalm 50:7-12; Acts 17:24-25.

Infinite—The realm of God has no limits or bounds whatsoever. 1 Kings 8:27; Psalm 145:3.

Transcendent—God is above His creation, and He would exist if there were no creation. His existence is totally apart from His creatures or creation. Isaiah 43:10; 55:8-9.

Sovereign—God is totally, supremely, and preeminently sovereign over all His creation. There is not a person or thing that is not under His control and foreknown plan. Daniel 4:35.

Holy—God is a morally excellent, perfect being. His being is pure in every aspect. Leviticus 19:2; Job 34:10; Isaiah 47:4; Isaiah 57:15.

Righteous—God is always good. It is essential to His character. He always does the right thing. Ultimately, since He is God, whatever He does is right. He is the absolute. His actions are always consistent with His character, which is love. Deuteronomy 32:4; Psalm 119:142.

Just—In all of His actions, God acts with fairness. Whether He deals with man, angels, or demons. He acts in total equity by rewarding righteousness and punishing sin. Since He knows all, every decree is absolutely just. Numbers 14:18; 23:19; Psalm 89:14.

Merciful—God is an actively compassionate being. He responds in a compassionate way toward those who have opposed His will in their pursuit of their own way. Psalm 62:12; 89:14; 116:5; Romans 9:14-16.

Long-suffering—God's righteous anger is slow to be kindled against those who fail to listen to His warnings or to obey His instructions. The eternal longing for the highest good for His creatures holds back His holy justice. Numbers 14:18; 2 Peter 3:9.

Wise—God's actions are based on His character, which allows Him to choose righteous ends and to make fitting plans to achieve those ends. Isaiah 40:28; Daniel 2:20.

Loving—This attribute of God causes Him to give Himself for another, even to the laying down of His own life. This attribute causes Him to desire the other's highest good without any thought for Himself. This love is not based upon the worth, response, or merit of the object being loved. Jeremiah 31:3; Romans 5:8; 1 John 4:8.

Good—This attribute of God causes Him to give to others in a way which has no motive and is not limited by what the recipients deserve. 2 Chronicles 5:13; Psalm 106:1.

Wrathful—There is within God a hatred for all that is unrighteous and an unquenchable desire to punish all unrighteousness. Whatever is inconsistent with Him must ultimately be consumed. Exodus 34:6-7; 2 Chronicles 19:2; Romans 1:18.

Truthful—All that God says is reality. Whether believed by man or not, whether seen as reality or not, if it is spoken by God, it is reality. Whatever He speaks becomes truth as we know it. Psalm 31:5; Titus 1:2.

Faithful—God is always true to His promises. He can never draw back from His promises of blessing or of judgment. Since He cannot lie, He is totally steadfast to what He has spoken. Deuteronomy 7:9; 2 Timothy 2:13.

Jealous—God is unwilling to share His glory with any other creature or give up His redeemed people. Exodus 20:5; 34:14.

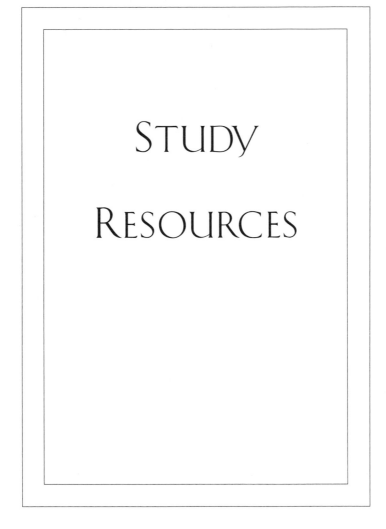

STUDY

RESOURCES

HOW TO MARK YOUR BIBLE

O ne of the things we at Precept Ministries International teach you to do in inductive Bible study is to find the key words in the passage you're studying and to mark them in a distinctive way. This is a very helpful and important element of the essential Bible study step known as observation—discovering exactly what the text says. So many times a Scripture passage is misinterpreted simply because the initial work of accurate observation has not been done. Remembering to mark key words will help you not to overlook this critical step.

WHAT ARE KEY WORDS?

Key words or phrases are those that are essential to the text. If they were to be removed, you would find it difficult or impossible to grasp the essence of what the passage is about. Like keys, these words "unlock" the meaning of the text. Recognizing them will help you uncover the author's intended purpose and emphasis in his message.

Key words can be nouns, descriptive words, or action words. Very often an author will repeat these words or phrases in order to emphasize his message. They may be repeated throughout an entire book—like the key words *love* and *abide,* which we see throughout the book of 1 John. Or they may be repeated throughout a shorter section of text, as with the key word *fellowship,* which is used four times in the first chapter of 1 John but not elsewhere in the book.

In the "Lord" series of Bible studies, you will often be asked to find and mark certain key words or phrases in the passage you're studying. This is a method that you will want to make a lifelong habit in your personal Bible study.

HOW TO MARK KEY WORDS

Marking key words can be done in several ways.

1. You can use different colors or a combination of colors to highlight

different words. When I mark a passage, I like to choose a color that to me best reflects the word I'm marking. I color references to God in yellow because God is light and in Him there is no darkness. I color sin brown. Any Old Testament reference to the temple is colored blue.

2. You can use a variety of symbols—simply drawing a circle around a word, underlining it, or marking it with a symbol of your own creation, such as these:

$$O \quad \triangle \quad \text{ }\sim\!\!\sim\!\!\sim\text{ } \quad \text{☁}$$

When I use symbols, I try to devise one that best pictures the word. For example, the key words *repent* and *repentance* in Matthew 3 might be marked with the symbol ⟿ since in Scripture this word's root meaning represents a change of mind, which often leads to a change in direction.

3. You can combine colors with symbols. For example:

• In 1 John 3, the key word *love* could be marked with a red heart like this: ♡ If you want to distinguish God's love from man's, you could color God's heart yellow and man's red.

• Every reference to the devil or evil spirits could be marked with a red pitchfork. ⚕

• Every occurrence of covenant could be colored red and boxed in with yellow.

The *New Inductive Study Bible* (NISB) has a whole page of suggested markings for key words used throughout the Bible.

A WORD OF CAUTION

When looking for key words, sometimes the tendency is to mark too many words. For example, I rarely mark references to God and to Jesus Christ unless it is significant to understanding the message. For instance, the phrases "in Christ" and "in Him" are significant to understanding the message of Ephesians 1–3. If you marked every reference to Jesus in some of the gospel accounts, your Bible would be too marked up. So you need to use discretion. (I always mark every reference to the Holy Spirit because He is not referred to often, and there is much confusion about the person and ministry of the Holy Spirit.)

Remember to look for those words that relate to the foundational theme of the text. Sometimes a key word may not be repeated frequently, but you know it is key because without it you would not know the essence of what the author is talking about in that passage.

BE SURE TO MARK KEY-WORD SYNONYMS AND PRONOUNS

Synonyms for a key word would be marked the same way you mark the key word. For example, you would mark identically the word *devil* and the phrase "evil one" in Ephesians 6:10-18.

And be sure to mark pronouns (I, you, he, she, it, we, our, and so on) the same way you would mark the words to which they refer. In 1 Timothy 3:1-7, for example, you would mark the pronouns *he* and *his* in the same way you did the key word *overseer* in that passage.

For consistency, you may want to list on an index card the key symbols and colors you like using for certain words and keep that card in your Bible.

IMMEDIATE IDENTIFICATION

With a passage's key words marked in this way, you can look at the text and immediately spot the word's usage and importance. In the future you'll quickly be able to track key subjects and identify significant truths in any passage you've studied and marked.

CREATE LISTS FROM KEY WORDS

After you mark key words, you will find it helpful to list what you learn from the text by the use of the key word. For instance, once you mark the word *sin* in 1 John 3, you would make a list of what the text tells you about sin. As you look at each marked key word, list anything that would answer the questions *who, what, when, where, why,* or *how* about sin. You will be not only surprised but also delighted at the truths you can learn from this simple process of observation.

For more on how to mark your Bible and on the inductive Bible study approach, you may want to use the *New Inductive Study Bible* (from Harvest House Publishers), or you can reach us at Precept Ministries International by referring to the contact information in the back of this book.

GUIDELINES FOR GROUP USE

This study book, as well as all those in the "Lord" series, can be used for home Bible-study groups, Sunday-school classes, family devotions, and a great variety of other group situations. Here are some things to keep in mind as you use this study in a group setting to minister to others.

- Prayerfully commit the entire study to the Lord, seeking His direction for every step.

- As your group forms, encourage each member to purchase an individual copy of this book.

- If you have the companion audio or videotapes for this course, begin your first class by listening to or viewing the introductory lesson on the study. Each student should then do the study preparation for chapter 1 before the next class. (Encourage each student to faithfully do this week by week.)

- Beginning with your next meeting, your weekly pattern as you meet should be to first discuss what you have all studied and learned on your own during the preceding week. Then, if you so desire, you could have a teacher present an in-depth message on the material you just studied. Or you could listen to or watch on video the teaching tapes available on this series. Just make sure that the teaching tape follows the class discussion rather than precedes it. You want your group to have the joy of discovery and discussion.

- The group discussion questions following each chapter in this book are to aid you in leading a discussion of that week's material. However, merely having these questions will not be enough for a really lively and successful discussion. The better you know your material, the greater freedom you will have in leading. Therefore, Beloved, be faithful in your own study and remain dependent upon the ministry of the Holy Spirit, who is there to lead you and guide you into all truth and who will enable you to fulfill the good work God has fore-ordained for you. (As the group's leader, it would be ideal if you could either read the entire book first or do several weeks' study in advance, so you know where you're going and can grasp the scope of the material covered in this study.)

• Each week as you prepare to lead the group's discussion, pray and ask the Father what your particular group needs to learn and how you can best cover the material. Pray with pen in hand. Make a list of what the Lord shows you. Then create your own questions or select from the questions at the end of each chapter, which will help stimulate and guide the group members in the Lord's direction within the time you have.

• Remember that your group members will find the greatest sense of accomplishment in discussing what they've learned in their own study, so try to stick to the subject at hand in your discussion. This will keep the class from becoming frustrated. Make sure the answers and insights come from the Word of God and are always in accordance with the whole counsel of God.

• Strive in your group to create an atmosphere of love, safety, and caring. Be concerned about one another. Bear one another's burdens and so fulfill the law of Christ—the law of love (Galatians 6:2). We desperately need one another.

Please know that I thank our Father for you and your willingness to assume this critical role of establishing God's people in God's Word. I know that this process produces glory and reverence for Him. So press on, valiant one. He is coming, bringing in the kingdom in all its glory, and His reward is with Him to give to each one of us according to our deeds.

THE "LORD" SERIES: AN OVERVIEW

My burden—and calling—is to help Christians (or interested or desperate inquirers) see for themselves what the Word of God has to teach on significant and relevant life-related subjects. So many people are weak and unstable in their Christianity because they don't know truth for themselves; they only know what others have taught them. These books, therefore, are designed to involve you in the incomparably enriching experience of daily study in God's Word.

Each book has been thoroughly tested and has already had an impact on a multitude of lives. Let me introduce the full series to you.

Lord, I Want to Know You is a foundational study for the "Lord" books. In this seventeen-week study you'll discover how God's character is revealed through His names, such as Creator, Healer, Protector, Provider, and many more. Within the names of God you'll encounter strength for your worst trials, comfort for your heart's deepest pain, and provision for your soul's greatest need. As you come to know Him more fully—the power of His glorious name and the depth of His infinite love—your walk with God will be transformed and your faith will be increased.

Lord, Heal My Hurts is, understandably, one of the most popular studies in this series. If you're in touch with the world, you know that people around you are in great pain. We run to many sources for relief when we are in pain. Some of us turn to other people; many escape into drugs, work, further education, and even hobbies. But in God you can find salvation from any situation, from any hurt. In this thirteen-week study you'll see that, no matter what you've done or what's been done to you, God wants to become your refuge…He loves you and desires your wholeness…and He offers healing for your deepest wounds.

Lord, I Need Grace to Make It Today will reveal to you in fresh power the amazing truth that God's grace is available for *every* situation, no matter how difficult, no matter how terrible. You'll gain the confidence that God will use you for His glory, as His grace enables you to persevere regardless of your need, regardless of your circumstances, and despite the backward pull of your flesh. You will see and know that the Lord and His all-sufficient grace will always be with you. A highlight of this nine-week course is your study of the book of Galatians and its liberating message about our freedom in Christ.

Lord, I'm Torn Between Two Masters opens your understanding to the kind of life that is truly pleasing to God. If you've known discouragement because you felt you could never measure up to God's standards or if you've ever felt unbearably stretched by the clash of life's priorities, this nine-week study of the Sermon on the Mount will lead you into a new freedom that will truly clear your vision and fortify your heart. You'll be encouraged to entwine your thoughts, hopes, dreams, and desires around heavenly things, and you'll find your life transformed by choosing to seek first God's kingdom and His righteousness.

Lord, Only You Can Change Me is an eight-week devotional study on character that draws especially on the so-called Beatitudes of Matthew 5. If you've ever been frustrated at not being all you wanted to be for the Lord or at not being able to change, you'll find in this study of Christ's teaching the path to true inner transformation that is accomplished only through the work of the indwelling Holy Spirit. You will learn the achievable reality of a godly life and the fulfillment it can bring.

Lord, Where Are You When Bad Things Happen is a critically important study in preparing you for times of trial. In this ten-week course you'll be grounded in the knowledge and confidence of God's sovereignty as you study especially the book of Habakkuk and see how God works in and through difficult and demanding situations. More than that, you'll learn what it means to live by faith…and to rest the details of your life in His hands.

Lord, Is It Warfare? Teach Me to Stand is a study that trains you for spiritual battle. God's Word tells us that our adversary, the devil, goes about like a roaring lion seeking whom he may devour (1 Peter 5:8). Many times we either don't recognize this enemy, or we're scared by his roar. We would like him to go away, but it's not that simple. In this eleven-week study you'll learn how to recognize Satan's tactics and how to be set free from bondage. As you focus your study especially on the book of Ephesians, you'll discover how to build an unshakable faith that makes victory yours for the taking. (This is the most challenging of the "Lord" books and requires an average of two to two and a half hours of weekly preparation to complete the assignments.)

Beloved, I have written these books so that you can have insight from God's Word on the pertinent issues of life—not only for yourself, but also for your ministry to others.

Know that you are on my heart because you are precious to God and I long to see you live as more than a conqueror, fulfilling God's purpose for your life.

On-Line Resources

A s you plant the seeds of God's Word in your heart in this study, I want you to know that you can now find immediate encouragement and help in a variety of ways just by connecting to our special "Lord" studies Web site at the address listed below.

Here's a sample listing of what you'll find at this site:

- Helpful information for guiding your individual study in this and other "Lord" books
- More detailed information on the exact study focus in all the "Lord" books
- Guidelines for group leaders and facilitators, both to get your group started and to keep it functioning in the best way
- Group study questions for you to download and reformat in a way that is most helpful for you and your group
- Additional insights on the topics in the "Lord" studies from the Precept Ministries International team
- Opportunities for you to join others in sharing your discoveries from God's Word

This information is continually updated to ensure that we're offering you the best support possible. Please e-mail and let us know what you find most helpful from this "Lord" studies Web site!

For more information on this and other "Lord" studies:
www.lordstudies.com
For other resources and information from Precept Ministries International:
www.precept.org

NOTES

CHAPTER TWO

1. From time to time we will look at the definition of a word in the Hebrew or Greek. Since the Old Testament was originally written in Hebrew and the New Testament was originally written in Koine Greek, sometimes it is helpful to go back to the original language to see the original meaning of a word. There are many study tools to help you if you would like to do this type of digging. One excellent book to help you understand how to do more in-depth study is *How to Study Your Bible* (Harvest House Publishers, 1994).

CHAPTER THREE

1. J. D. Douglas, *The New Bible Dictionary* (Grand Rapids, Mich.: Wm. B. Eerdmans Publishing Co., 1962), 469.
2. Marvin R. Vincent, *Word Studies in the New Testament,* vol. 4 (Grand Rapids, Mich.: Wm. B. Eerdmans Publishing Company, 1969), 318.
3. Vincent, *Word Studies,* 318.

CHAPTER FOUR

1. If you are not aware of all that Jesus endured for you at Calvary so that you could be saved and healed, and if you are not using the videos that accompany this study, I urge you to rent our video on this lesson. It has ministered greatly to many.

CHAPTER NINE

1. These are words which God gave to Jerusalem, the city and home of His covenant people—this is who "Zion" is. If Isaiah 49:14-16 is a word to Jerusalem, it is a word to the nation of Israel. If it is a word to them, it is a word to you in the light of the Crucifixion and the New Covenant of grace.

CHAPTER TEN

1. You might find it profitable to start your own notebook. As you read through God's Word day by day, record those scriptures which specifically apply to your position in Christ, your personal hurts, needs, or misconceptions of God. Go over what you have written, read it aloud, and embrace it in faith. Remember to personalize each verse, putting your name in place of each pronoun that refers to a child of God.

   Let me give you an example. I might take Colossians 2:9-14: "For in Him all the fulness of Deity dwells in bodily form, and in Him Kay (use your name!) has been made complete, and He is the head over all rule and authority;...having been buried with Him in baptism...Kay was also raised up with Him through faith in the working of God.... He made Kay alive together with Him, having forgiven Kay *all* her transgressions. Oh God, I'm complete in you—I need nothing else. I'm alive in You, and I want to live Your life to its fullest. I'm forgiven for everything."

Don't forget to savor each truth!

2. If you don't know what your spiritual gifts are, you might want to do our Precept Bible Study course on spiritual gifts. Simply write: Precept Ministries International; P.O. Box 182218; Chattanooga, TN 37422-7218; or call (423) 892-6814.

CHAPTER TWELVE

1. As we begin our study on anger, I think it will be profitable for you to have a good understanding of the word *anger* and how it is translated in the Old and New Testaments.

Some of the insights I want to share with you have been gleaned from Lawrence Richards's enlightening and helpful book *Expository Dictionary of Bible Words*. If you don't have this book, you should. It is a treasure.

There are a variety of words in the Old Testament which express anger. The most common Old Testament words for anger are the verb *kaas* and the noun *ap*. *Kaas* is often used to describe God's anger.

Qasap, the verb, and *qesep*, the noun, are often translated *wrath* and are the strongest terms for anger in the Old Testament. *Qasap* "focuses attention on the relational damage done when one party has said or done something that causes hot anger or deep displeasure." Lawrence O. Richards, *Expository Dictionary of Bible Words*, Regency Reference Library (Grand Rapids, Mich.: Zondervan, 1985), 46.

The Old Testament words *hemah* and *haron* mean "burning" and describe anger as "heated emotional passion."

The word *ebrah* means "an overflow" or "fury." This word lays stress on the fierceness of the anger. Used of human anger, it suggests "an arrogant pride expressed as implacable fury." (Richards, *Expository Dictionary*, 46.)

The Greek word which is translated *anger* in the New Testament is the word *orgē* and is understood in contrast to the word *thumos* which is translated *wrath*. When you study Ephesians 4:31—"Let all bitterness and wrath and anger and clamor and slander be put away from you, along with all malice"—you see wrath and anger used side by side.

W. E. Vine, in his *Expository Dictionary of Biblical Words*, says, "*Thumos*, wrath (not translated "anger"), is to be distinguished from *orgē*, in this respect, that *thumos* indicates a more agitated condition of the feelings, an outburst of wrath from inward indignation, while *orgē* suggests a more settled or abiding condition of mind, frequently with a view to taking revenge. *Orgē* is less sudden in its rise than *thumos*, but more lasting in its nature. *Thumos* expresses more the inward feeling, *orgē* the more active emotion. *Thumos* may issue in revenge, though it does not necessarily include it. It is characteristic that it quickly blazes up and quickly subsides though that is not necessarily implied in each case." W. E. Vine, *Expository Dictionary of Biblical Words*, 3d ed., (Nashville: Thomas Nelson, 1984), 47-48.

It is apparent that anger is an emotion which occurs because of some event which takes place. In other words, anger is an inward emotion evoked by an outward action, circumstance, or situation. The action, circumstance, or situation may be something we do or fail to do, or it may be something done apart from us or done to us.

CHAPTER THIRTEEN

1. Vine describes meekness as "an inwrought grace of the soul; and the exercises of it are first and chiefly towards God. It is that temper of spirit in which we accept His dealings with us as good, and therefore without disputing and resisting." W. E. Vine, *Expository Dictionary of New Testament Words,* 3d ed., (Nashville: Thomas Nelson Publishers, 1983), 727.
2. The NASB translates *meek* and *meekness* as "gentle" or "gentleness" in the New Testament, while in the Old Testament it is translated "humble" or "afflicted."
3. This tape can be ordered through Precept Ministries.

About Kay Arthur and
Precept Ministries International

Kay Arthur, executive vice president and cofounder of Precept Ministries International, is known around the world as a Bible teacher, author, conference speaker, former missionary, and host of national radio and television programs.

Kay and her husband, Jack, founded Precept Ministries in 1970 in Chattanooga, Tennessee. Started as a fledgling ministry for teens, Precept today is a worldwide outreach that establishes children, teens, and adults in God's Word, so that they can discover the Bible's truths for themselves. Precept inductive Bible studies are taught in all 50 states. The studies have been translated into 60 languages, reaching 118 countries.

Kay is the author of more than 40 books and 27 inductive Bible study courses, with a total of over 5 million books in print. She is sought after by groups throughout the world as an inspiring Bible teacher and conference speaker. Kay is also well known globally through her daily and weekly television programs that air regularly on over 900 stations in 30 countries.

Contact Precept Ministries for more information about inductive Bible studies in your area.

Precept Ministries International
P.O. Box 182218
Chattanooga, TN 37422-7218
800-763-8280
www.precept.org